OPPOSING VIEWPOINTS® SERIES

Gentrification and the Housing Crisis

Marcia Amidon Lusted, Book Editor

GREENHAVEN
PUBLISHING

Published in 2019 by Greenhaven Publishing, LLC
353 3rd Avenue, Suite 255, New York, NY 10010

Copyright © 2019 by Greenhaven Publishing, LLC

First Edition

Cover image: HipKat/Shutterstock.com

Library of Congress Cataloging-in-Publication Data

Names: Lusted, Marcia Amidon, editor.
Title: Gentrification and the housing crisis / Marcia Amidon Lusted, book
  editor.
Description: First edition. | New York: Greenhaven Publishing, 2019. |
  Series: Opposing viewpoints | Includes bibliographical references and
  index. | Audience: Grades 9-12.
Identifiers: LCCN 2018021200| ISBN 9781534504127 (library bound) | ISBN
  9781534504356 (pbk.)
Subjects: LCSH: Gentrification—United States—Juvenile literature. | Urban
  renewal—United States—Juvenile literature. | Housing—United
  States—Juvenile literature.
Classification: LCC HT175 .G469 2019 | DDC 307.3/4160973—dc23
LC record available at https://lccn.loc.gov/2018021200

Manufactured in the United States of America

Website: http://greenhavenpublishing.com

Contents

Chapter 3: Does Gentrification Diminish a Community's History and Culture?

Chapter 4: Does Gentrification Have Economic Benefits?

The Importance of Opposing Viewpoints

P erhaps every generation experiences a period in time in which the populace seems especially polarized, starkly divided on the important issues of the day and gravitating toward the far ends of the political spectrum and away from a consensus-facilitating middle ground. The world that today's students are growing up in and that they will soon enter into as active and engaged citizens is deeply fragmented in just this way. Issues relating to terrorism, immigration, women's rights, minority rights, race relations, health care, taxation, wealth and poverty, the environment, policing, military intervention, the proper role of government—in some ways, perennial issues that are freshly and uniquely urgent and vital with each new generation—are currently roiling the world.

If we are to foster a knowledgeable, responsible, active, and engaged citizenry among today's youth, we must provide them with the intellectual, interpretive, and critical-thinking tools and experience necessary to make sense of the world around them and of the all-important debates and arguments that inform it. After all, the outcome of these debates will in large measure determine the future course, prospects, and outcomes of the world and its peoples, particularly its youth. If they are to become successful members of society and productive and informed citizens, students need to learn how to evaluate the strengths and weaknesses of someone else's arguments, how to sift fact from opinion and fallacy, and how to test the relative merits and validity of their own opinions against the known facts and the best possible available information. The landmark series Opposing Viewpoints has been providing students with just such critical-thinking skills and exposure to the debates surrounding society's most urgent contemporary issues for many years, and it continues to serve this essential role with undiminished commitment, care, and rigor.

The key to the series's success in achieving its goal of sharpening students' critical-thinking and analytic skills resides in its title—

Opposing Viewpoints. In every intriguing, compelling, and engaging volume of this series, readers are presented with the widest possible spectrum of distinct viewpoints, expert opinions, and informed argumentation and commentary, supplied by some of today's leading academics, thinkers, analysts, politicians, policy makers, economists, activists, change agents, and advocates. Every opinion and argument anthologized here is presented objectively and accorded respect. There is no editorializing in any introductory text or in the arrangement and order of the pieces. No piece is included as a "straw man," an easy ideological target for cheap point-scoring. As wide and inclusive a range of viewpoints as possible is offered, with no privileging of one particular political ideology or cultural perspective over another. It is left to each individual reader to evaluate the relative merits of each argument— as he or she sees it, and with the use of ever-growing critical-thinking skills—and grapple with his or her own assumptions, beliefs, and perspectives to determine how convincing or successful any given argument is and how the reader's own stance on the issue may be modified or altered in response to it.

This process is facilitated and supported by volume, chapter, and selection introductions that provide readers with the essential context they need to begin engaging with the spotlighted issues, the debates surrounding them, and their own perhaps shifting or nascent opinions on them. In addition, guided reading and discussion questions encourage readers to determine the authors' point of view and purpose, interrogate and analyze the various arguments and their rhetoric and structure, evaluate the arguments' strengths and weaknesses, test their claims against available facts and evidence, judge the validity of the reasoning, and bring into clearer, sharper focus the reader's own beliefs and conclusions and how they may differ from or align with those in the collection or those of their classmates.

Research has shown that reading comprehension skills improve dramatically when students are provided with compelling, intriguing, and relevant "discussable" texts. The subject matter of these collections could not be more compelling, intriguing, or urgently relevant to today's students and the world they are poised to inherit. The anthologized articles and the reading and discussion questions that are included with them also provide the basis for stimulating, lively, and passionate classroom debates. Students who are compelled to anticipate objections to their own argument and identify the flaws in those of an opponent read more carefully, think more critically, and steep themselves in relevant context, facts, and information more thoroughly. In short, using discussable text of the kind provided by every single volume in the Opposing Viewpoints series encourages close reading, facilitates reading comprehension, fosters research, strengthens critical thinking, and greatly enlivens and energizes classroom discussion and participation. The entire learning process is deepened, extended, and strengthened.

For all of these reasons, Opposing Viewpoints continues to be exactly the right resource at exactly the right time—when we most need to provide readers with the critical-thinking tools and skills that will serve them well not only in school but also in their careers and their daily lives as decision-making family members, community members, and citizens. This series encourages respectful engagement with and analysis of opposing viewpoints and fosters a resulting increase in the strength and rigor of one's own opinions and stances. In these ways, it helps make readers "future ready," and that readiness will pay rich dividends for the readers themselves, the citizenry, our society, and the world at large.

Introduction

During the twentieth century in the United States, it often seemed as if people were moving out of cities as fast as they could, for better lives in suburbs and rural areas. But now, in the twenty-first century, the ideal is quite the opposite. It may be because of the availability of good jobs or perhaps because cities offer so many varied forms of entertainment and cultural advantages. Recent college graduates flock to urban areas, where there are more opportunities. After a while, they may even raise their families there. Some empty nesters are moving back to urban environments where they might have lived as college students or young professionals. In a 2015 survey, the US Census Bureau found that while cities make up just 3.5 percent of the land in the United States, almost 63 percent of the country's population lives in a city.

For whatever reason, more people are looking for interesting and affordable neighborhoods in cities or places that seem to be on the edge of becoming the next revitalized or popular place to live. This is often referred to as urban revival, when older neighborhoods suddenly see an influx of new residents. Some neighborhoods are attractive because, unlike the suburbs or small towns, they are walkable and don't require a car to access stores, entertainment, and jobs. Young, single professionals like city neighborhoods because of the variety of places to eat, drink, and find entertainment. But what often happens when new, often more affluent people move into an existing neighborhood is that housing becomes in short supply, and landlords can charge higher rents. Residents who have lived in these neighborhoods for a long time suddenly find that they can't afford to pay the higher rents, and they either struggle to adjust or leave their homes.

In addition to bringing in new residents and higher real estate prices, this transition can also change the flavor of the neighborhood. Trendy new bars, restaurants, and coffee shops open, sometimes pushing out the mom-and-pop stores that have been there for years and making it more difficult to access the everyday products and services that used to be there. The cultural identity of the neighborhood may change as well, as ethnic communities and their support systems crumble as people are forced to move away.

This whole process of newcomers moving into neighborhoods, often changing the areas' identity and displacing the older residents, is known as *gentrification*. The word was coined by British sociologist Ruth Glass in 1964, based on the changes she had observed in the city of London:

> One by one, many of the working class quarters have been invaded by the middle class—upper and lower. Shabby, modest mews and cottages—two rooms up and two down—have been taken over, when their leases have expired, and have become elegant, expensive residences ... Once this process of "gentrification" starts in a district it goes on rapidly until all or most of the working class occupiers are displaced and the whole social character of the district is changed.

However, those who study urban environments and the effects of gentrification point out that it is not always a bad thing. It can raise the value of homes, so that established residents who own their own houses may find that their property values have increased a great deal. It can bring more jobs into the immediate neighborhood and often improved schools and public services as well. Gentrification can encourage historical preservation, saving culturally and historically important structures and areas from neglect or demolition. Gentrification an also create more vital, racially and economically mixed neighborhoods.

In chapters titled "Does Gentrification Help Improve Urban Environments?," "Does Gentrification Contribute to the Housing Crisis?," "Does Gentrification Diminish a Community's History and Culture?," and "Does Gentrification Have Economic Benefits?," *Opposing Viewpoints: Gentrification and the Housing Crisis* explores the complexities of gentrification, both the positive and the negative, the successful communities where new residents are integrated, and those that displace their original residents and leave them struggling to survive and with nowhere to go. As the trend of populations moving into urban areas increases—a trend that is taking place all over the world—addressing gentrification will become even more vital.

CHAPTER 1

Does Gentrification Help Improve Urban Environments?

Chapter Preface

O ne of the biggest controversies of gentrification is whether it can help improve urban environments. There are arguments that the process of bringing new residents into a neighborhood community, residents who often have more money to use for housing and to spend on their lifestyle, can only help a neighborhood. These new residents will attract better businesses, create new amenities such as parks and green spaces, improve schools, and invite new jobs. Newly gentrified neighborhoods may have an increased police presence, lowering crime rates.

However, the other side of the argument states that many of the new features brought to gentrified neighborhoods are of no use to its original residents. Working-class residents may have no use for a bike path or a new green space within their neighborhood and may not be able to afford expensive coffee or organic groceries when they become the only options. Gentrification may mean the destruction of affordable housing units, with nothing to replace them, and may drive out long-standing neighborhood businesses when they can no longer pay the rental rates that trendy new businesses can afford. Often gentrification is seen as displacing minorities to an unfair degree. It may even make these populations a target for law enforcement and police violence, whereas they were once part of the social fabric and ethnic makeup of their neighborhoods and weren't viewed with distrust simply on account of race. Gentrification can create polarized neighborhoods, with wealthy newcomers living in gorgeously renovated homes or newly built condos or apartments, separated from the daily life of the neighborhood as it once was.

> *"When neighborhoods undergo meaningful economic and social changes, like those that transpire under gentrification, there are surely implications for the local business environment."*

The Results of Gentrification Are Mixed

Rachel Meltzer

In the following excerpted viewpoint, Rachel Meltzer argues that despite the common assumption that gentrification will threaten the existence of a neighborhood's small businesses, the reality is that this is not always true. Gentrification can bring new opportunities for small businesses, and data shows that the rate of small businesses leaving or staying in a neighborhood is the same whether that neighborhood gentrifies or not. Meltzer is an assistant professor of urban policy and chair of the Public and Urban Policy Program at the New School in New York City.

As you read, consider the following questions:

1. What important roles does the "corner store" play in a neighborhood?
2. What kinds of changes do small businesses see because of gentrification?
3. What advantages are there for small businesses when their location becomes gentrified?

"Gentrification and Small Business: Threat or Opportunity?" by Rachel Meltzer, US Department of Housing and Urban Development, July 13, 2016.

L ocal, small businesses are very much tied to their surrounding communities. Therefore, when neighborhoods undergo meaningful economic and social changes, such as those that take place under gentrification, one would expect local businesses to feel the effects. But is gentrification a threat or a boon for existing businesses? And what are the implications for the residents that patronize these services? I test these questions here, using microdata on properties and businesses in New York City. I also drill down to three illustrative case neighborhoods, which reveal nuance beyond the average citywide effects. The results are mixed, and show that gentrification is associated with both business retention and disruption. I find that the majority of businesses stay in place, and displacement is no more prevalent in the typical gentrifying neighborhood. However, when businesses do leave gentrifying neighborhoods, their spaces tend to sit vacant for relatively longer periods of time. Gentrifying neighborhoods are more likely to attract new types of services than non-gentrifying and higher-income neighborhoods; and they more often attract chains to replace displaced businesses. However, as the neighborhood drill-downs show, there are still cases where neighborhoods undergoing gentrification lose businesses without the upside of new amenities.

Introduction

Much of the literature on gentrification has focused on how it impacts residents and housing. However, we know that the nature and quality of neighborhoods, especially those in urban settings, are also determined by the commercial enterprises that serve the community. The "corner store," an emblem of local retail, has long played an important economic and cultural role in neighborhood development and livelihood (Liebow, 1967). Retail services, particularly in mixed-use settings, not only provide material needs for those living nearby, but less-tangible social and cultural capital as well (Zukin et al., 2009; Hyra, 2008; Deener, 2007). Therefore, it follows that when neighborhoods undergo meaningful economic and social changes, like those that transpire under gentrification, there are surely implications for the local business environment. These potential changes are important not only for the business proprietors, but also for the residents that patronize their services and consume their goods.

We know that business location decisions, and their subsequent survival, are a function of the existing (and potential) consumer base in an area (Meltzer and Schuetz, 2012; Waldfogel, 2008). A gentrification-induced shift in its composition, certainly economically and often racially/ethnically, could mean several things for local businesses. These changes could be a boon for local businesses, if they bring in new consumers; however, if the new consumers also have different tastes and usher in higher rents, then the incumbent businesses could suffer. For residents, the prospect of new services, new employment opportunities and street vitality are weighed against the potential interruption in the culture and services on which they had historically relied.

[...]

I find that gentrification can bring both opportunities and threats, for the businesses and the community more generally. Citywide, the majority of businesses stay in place over time. Furthermore, the rate of displacement/retention is no different across gentrifying and non-gentrifying neighborhoods. However, when businesses do leave gentrifying neighborhoods, their spaces tend to sit vacant for relatively longer periods of time. Gentrifying neighborhoods more often attract chains to replace displaced businesses than non-gentrifying and higher-income neighborhoods and are more likely to attract services different than those that operated in the neighborhood prior to gentrification. However, as the neighborhood drill-downs show, there are still cases where neighborhoods undergoing gentrification lose businesses without the upside of new amenities.

Neighborhood-Based Small Businesses

Historically, small, local businesses have played an important role in the cultural and economic capital of urban neighborhoods. Prior to the 1970s, before inner cities faced decades of disinvestment, local businesses, like corner stores, markets and eateries, were a central part of the neighborhood's fabric (Ehrenhalt, 1999; Oldenberg, 1999 and 2002; Lloyd, 2010; Sutton, 2010). In addition, they have long been considered a vehicle for entrepreneurship, especially among minority and immigrant populations (Sutton, 2010; Fairlie, 2012). These neighborhood businesses epitomize "local" not only in terms of their consumer base and proprietors (many of whom often come from the immediate community), but also their cultural and economic reach (Hyra, 2015; Hyra, 2008). This geographic immediacy, of their inputs and outputs, is consistent with Jacobs' argument (1961) that local small businesses are not only good for services and access to jobs, but are critical to the vitality of community life.

What Happens to Businesses When Neighborhoods Gentrify?

Patch (2008) suggests that retail change, or "street gentrification," is an important harbinger of broader socioeconomic trends that has thus far been under-appreciated. Gentrification, a term coined by Glass (1964), originally referred to a phenomenon of socioeconomic transition: one where more affluent and more educated "gentry" enter a low-income neighborhood. These changes can bring new services and access to a wider choice of basic goods, more vital and safer streets and even local employment opportunities. However, gentrification can also disrupt commercially-driven neighborhood identities and introduce services and products that do not serve incumbent residents. The commercial activity and residential composition of a neighborhood are closely tied, and, when a neighborhood gentrifies, the consumer base and costs of operation for a local business can shift as well (Meltzer and Schuetz, 2012; Zukin, 2008; Carree and Thurik, 1996; Hotelling, 1929).

Businesses: Changes in Consumer Demand

For existing businesses, a new pool of local residents could mean both more and less patronage. Waldfogel (2008) shows that preferences for retail services are strongly correlated with observable population characteristics, such as income, educational attainment and race/ethnicity. There is also empirical evidence to show that household residential preferences are influenced by local amenities, like commercial services (Meltzer and Capperis, 2016; Kolko, 2011). If, on net, the local consumer base has tastes that do not align with the services or goods that existing establishments provide, then local businesses could suffer. On the other hand, new residential activity could be a stabilizing force if it provides an injection of cash flow that the neighborhood was previously lacking. In addition, these socio-economic changes could draw new businesses and services into the neighborhood.

Businesses: Changes in Start-Up and Operating Costs

Gentrification can also change the costs of operating or opening up a business. For existing businesses, the effect is very direct: due to increased demand for the area, rents can increase. Without a concomitant increase in revenues, the costs of operating could become unsustainable and force closure. It is important to note, that the pressures from rising commercial rents can take a different form than residential ones. Commercial leases tend to be much longer than residential ones (Genesove, 2003; Mooradian and Yang, 2000), and therefore businesses can often sustain operations at the original, lower rents as properties in the neighborhood otherwise appreciate. Therefore, any displacement could take longer to transpire. Rising rents (and new investments more broadly) can also influence the kinds of businesses that opt into the neighborhood, and by association, the range and prices of products that they sell. Alternatively, higher rents can also deter entry, leaving vacated commercial spaces empty for sustained periods of time.

[...]

In conclusion, there does appear to be opportunity for the neighborhoods that gain quality-of-life services and that retain more businesses under conditions of gentrification—perhaps due to new and increased spending power locally. The threats are also palpable: the displacement that does occur can leave gentrifying neighborhoods with disproportionately more vacant spaces and without the promise of new amenities. And even in the neighborhoods where services grow and/or change, the new products, price points or cultural orientation could be more alienating than useful for incumbent residents. Therefore, even in the absence of systematic business displacement, gentrification can present challenges around the management of changing neighborhood services. Here, neighborhood-based organizations, like Business Improvement Districts and community development corporations, and real estate brokers can play a role in coordinating input from the community and conveying it to property owners. Moreover, new investment, which tends to happen in gentrifying neighborhoods, provides a critical opportunity for local government to negotiate the terms of development, including where commercial space is created and how it is used. This approach has increasingly been used with housing, where permitting or zoning allowances are contingent on affordable housing provision—a similar approach can be applied to the provision of commercial space and services.

| "In order to succeed in any aspect of life, people and businesses have to adapt to change."

Small Businesses Are Being Driven Out of Their Neighborhoods

Abigail Savitch-Lew

In the following viewpoint, Abigail Savitch-Lew argues the need for a Small Business Jobs Survival Act. Among other measures, this act would put in place rights such as a ten-year lease for commercial tenants and the right to have any new rental rate subject to arbitration. The goal is to help small businesses find and keep affordable rental spaces even in places where gentrification is causing rent increases that often drive out a neighborhood's indigenous small businesses. Savitch-Lew is a staff reporter for City Limits, an investigative nonprofit news agency that reports on urban issues pertinent to New York City.

As you read, consider the following questions:

1. What legal and constitutional issues might result from the proposed rental bill?
2. What is "the right of first refusal," and why is it important?
3. Why might a rent-control bill be bad for new businesses?

"Trepidation Around Proposal for Regulating Store Rents in NYC," by Abigail Savitch-Lew, City Limits, June 13, 2016. Reprinted by permission.

I t is no secret that retail lease rates are skyrocketing throughout the city and that it's taking a toll on small businesses. On some streets in Brooklyn, commercial rents increased about 40 percent between June 2014 and 2015, while in 2014 the Bronx led the city with a 30 percent increase in court-ordered commercial evictions. A variety of solutions have been proposed to address the crisis, from zoning restrictions on chain stores to the provision of below-market commercial space in city-sponsored developments. Still others argue there's only one real solution: establishing a right to lease renewal.

The long-sought Small Business Jobs Survival Act, which would establish such a right, has been kicking around City Council for three decades. Though it has the support of a diverse coalition, from the Small Business Congress to the Artists Affordability Project, it remains stalled in committee, its progress hampered by questions about the bill's legality, economic concerns and the strong opposition of the real estate lobby.

The bill would give any tenant of a commercial space, whether they are a corner bodega, a chain pharmacy, a medical office or an arts nonprofit, the right to a 10-year lease, or a shorter lease with the tenant's agreement. The landlord must renew that lease unless he or she has sufficient grounds to refuse, such as evidence that the tenant is regularly late with rent or because the owner wants to reoccupy their property.

When the lease comes up for renewal, the landlord and tenant would negotiate a new rent, or, if they couldn't agree, present their cases to an independent arbitrator who would determine the rent based on over a dozen criteria, including comparable rents in the area, the landlords' expenses, the nature of the tenant's business, how much the business is bound to a particular location and other factors.

The law also gives tenants the "right of first refusal," meaning that if the tenant doesn't accept the arbitrator's designated rent and the landlord proceeds to seek a new tenant, the existing tenant is given the option to stay in the space paying the rent amount

DIVERSITY OVER GENTRIFICATION

This Tuesday and Wednesday I went to a conference for Smart Growth in Pittsburgh. At the conference, a local documentary filmmaker—Chris Ivey—presented a few clips of his documentary series: *East of Liberty.*

East of Liberty covers some raw topics that developers interested in urban renewal don't like to talk about much: gentrification and low-income residents. As plenty of post-industrial Great Lakes cities (not just Pittsburgh—where *East of Liberty* was shot) draw up plans for revitalizing their urban cores, we must take into account the current residents of those spaces.

While it may seem that bringing in new businesses and nicer apartment buildings is good for these cities, they often raise realty prices and property taxes, pushing low- and moderate-income residents out of the newly developed spaces. Often, no alternatives or quality low-income housing arrangements are made for these urban refugees.

Urban renewal does not have to mean gentrification. Low- and moderate-income people deserve safe and family-friendly neighborhoods as much as anyone else. If we want to re-develop existing communities, then we should engage the people who live there in the planning process and offer low-income housing options in those developments.

In areas where developers work on integrating housing of different price ranges (think of the west side of Cleveland), there can be a rich diversity that renders vibrant neighborhoods.

And if you're worried about safety, then invest in a quality police force that will protect all of the residents who live there.

"Urban Renewal Does Not Have to Mean Gentrification," Renovating the Rust Belt, March 26, 2010.

proposed by the prospective new tenant. If the tenant decided to move or the business failed before the lease was up, laws already in effect would apply: The landlord could sue to recover any money owed, and the tenant could try to lessen their dues by helping the landlord find a new tenant.

Constitutional Questions

Supporters of SBJSA say safeguarding small businesses from displacement would benefit entire low-income communities by protecting local jobs, preventing the extortion of immigrant business owners, and preserving affordable, culturally-appropriate services. Opponents argue the bill would interfere with the natural evolution of neighborhoods, discourage businesses from investing in their expansion and violate the constitution.

"The city's dynamism, in part, is driven by its ever-changing population, building stock and mix of businesses. Understandably, some don't like change," said John Banks, the president of the Real Estate Board of New York (REBNY) in a statement sent to City Limits. "However, such feelings don't justify unconstitutional legislation like the Small Business Jobs Survival Act."

It is not unreasonable to question the bill's legality. Its supporters admit that such a policy does not exist anywhere else in the United States, and in 1987 a similar bill in Berkeley, Calif., was found illegal by a federal court and overturned. Advocates, however, claim that an independent legal review of SBJSA conducted in 2010 showed the bill was legal and did not include the same fault as the Berkeley bill, which didn't give owners the right to reclaim their property for their own use.

But some are not convinced. Though the bill is co-sponsored by 27 City Council members and the Public Advocate—more than enough needed to become law—continued doubts about the bill's legality keep it from getting a hearing.

In June 2015, a year after Bronx Councilmember Annabel Palma reintroduced the bill, Speaker Melissa Mark-Viverito told *The Villager* that Council staff first needed to "do their due diligence" and look over the bill, after which it would receive a hearing. She added that there are some bills that "legally we don't have the ability to implement as a city."

One year later, there are no updates available from the legislative division and no hearing has been scheduled. Meanwhile, Councilmembers Jumaane Williams and Brad Lander—early supporters of the bill—have both withdrawn their sponsorship. Some sources, who spoke on background, told City Limits there were concerns because rent regulation is within the state's, not the city's, jurisdiction.

Advocates for the bill say neither City Council or REBNY has ever responded to the findings of the 2010 panel, which determined that there were no legal issues with the bill, and that the city did have the authority to rule on the matter.

"What are the legal issues? … Please tell us what they are," says Ahmad El-Najjar, a representative of Take Back NYC, a coalition of small businesses and community advocates fighting for SBJSA. "No one has ever provided any document that actually cite what the actual legal issues are. Not one. It's a talking point."

Impact of Residential Rents?

Palma, meanwhile, says she is very frustrated with the delay. "This bill has been around for decades and analyzed by various lawyers I know. It is perhaps the most scrutinized bill before the council. As a result, I believe this bill is legally sound," she said in an e-mail to City Limits. "The Bronx is the last frontier in terms of development, and we have the opportunity to learn from the fast-paced economic and developmental changes that have occurred in Brooklyn and Queens."

She added that because no members of the Small Business Committee have signed on in support of the bill, she is working to acquire a total of 34 sponsors, the number required to mandate a hearing.

In a statement sent to City Limits on Wednesday morning, City Hall offered a straightforward rejection of the bill.

"The administration recognizes the growing challenges small businesses face finding space they can afford, but has not supported commercial rent control. We are working to lower small businesses' costs in other ways," said Raul Contreras, assistant press secretary for the mayor. The administration is concerned that if commercial rents are decided through arbitration, landlords of mixed-use buildings might raise the rents of residential tenants to compensate for the profits they could not make from commercial tenants. Contreras listed a variety of other measures that the city is taking to reduce the burden on small businesses, including streamlining regulations, reducing fines and providing pro-bono legal services to help businesses negotiate their leases.

Advocates, however, insist the administration is mischaracterizing the bill in a way that raises irrelevant ideological questions.

"This is not rent control," says El-Najjar. "It's just the right to a fair lease negotiation. It should never be confused with rent control." Addressing the administration's concerns that landlords will jack up residential rents, El-Najjar says that mixed-use properties make up a small percentage of the residential market and that in such buildings landlords are already charging residential tenants as much as the market can bear or, if the apartments are rent-stabilized, charge as much as the Rent Guidelines Board will allow.

"I give [the administration] credit for framing this in a way that attempts to drive a wedge between commercial and residential tenants," he says.

A Long History of Debate

While much of the country considers any kind of rent regulation unconstitutional, New York City has a long—if embattled—history of embracing residential rent regulation. The city's equally long fight over commercial rent regulation is not as well known, though perhaps even more controversial. While some free-market adherents oppose any interference, those who support residential rent regulation but are leery of the commercial version note that it would effectively subsidize private businesses, which, unlike residents, stand to make a profit off an area's increasing popularity.

New York did have actual commercial rent control once: In 1945, responding to the wartime emergency that had spurred skyrocketing rents and eviction rates, the New York State legislature enacted a law that limited when a commercial tenant could be evicted and instituted restrictions on rent increases. Landlords could not raise rents by more than 15 percent above 1943 or 1944 rent levels if it would lead to a profit of more than 8 percent. The law was challenged repeatedly in the courts, and ultimately the legislature allowed it to expire in 1963.

In the 1980s, as small business owners began to suffer from the city's first wave of gentrification, some elected officials and advocates once again took up the discussion of commercial rent regulation, and the Koch administration established a commission to study the problem. A draft of SBJSA emerged from the commission's work and immediately became the subject of heated debate. In 1988, it received its first and last City Council committee vote—rejected by a 4 to 3 count.

Both in 1988 and when SBJSA was reintroduced in 2008, City Council members and legislative staff asked questions about the bill's legality. There were concerns that the bill violated the constitutions' "contract" clause, which forbids the government from "impairing" contracts between private individuals. The bill overturned in Berkeley in 1987 was scrapped for violating that clause. There were further concerns that the bill would violate the "takings" clause, which forbids the government from taking private property without just compensation—a clause also regularly cited in legal arguments against residential rent control. Restricting a landlord's ability to hike rents, the thinking goes, effectively snatches away some of the value embedded in their real-estate asset. City Council members also questioned whether the city had the authority to make such a regulation, but corporation counsel lawyers in 1988 and the City Counsel legislative division in 2009 both concluded that the city did, in fact, have jurisdiction.

An independent panel of lawyers, including the Urban Justice Center's Edward Barbieri, former Justice of the NYS Supreme Court Karen Smith and others, convened in 2010 to examine these concerns. They found that the Berkeley law had been found in violation of the contracts clause because it did not give owners the right to retake their property, while SBJSA did. They argued that SBJSA did not constitute an "impairment" of a contract, only a procedure for the renewal of contracts.

Furthermore, they agreed that prior court decisions held that such a policy was not in violation of the takings clause because the landlord would always receive "fair compensation" in the form of the new rent amount. And, agreeing with the city's own lawyers, they stated that City Council had "home rule": Only the state could institute residential rent control, but the city had a right to regulate commercial contracts.

Bad for Business?

Even if the bill is legally sound, there are some who believe it would bring disastrous consequences—not only for landlords, but for small businesses and communities as well.

"The SBSJA is incredibly disadvantageous to new and growing businesses, which are vital to the city's growth and expansion," argues James O'Neill, an associate of the real estate and business services organization CPEX Real Estate, in a March op-ed. Because existing businesses would have the right to 10-year leases, he argues, there would be limited available space for new entrepreneurs. Old businesses would have no incentive to improve their stores by reinvesting in growth and improvement because they'd have no ability to rent new space to expand. He also worries the legislation would deter the creation of healthy, thriving neighborhoods.

"As communities grow and change, businesses that are priced out of hot commercial strips move to the periphery of the neighborhood, bringing exciting new shops and services to these areas," O'Neill continues. "In order to succeed in any aspect of life, people and businesses have to adapt to change, and it should not be the government's role to foster stagnation."

On the flip side, others have noted that the bill won't stop neighborhood businesses from becoming less affordable to low-income residents: there's nothing in the bill to prevent the people who operate the local bodega from shifting to a gourmet grocer. The profits that come from servicing an increasingly wealthy population would merely go to the business owner instead of the landlord.

Responding to these critiques, El-Najjar of Take Back NYC said he did not believe the bill would cause economic stagnation, because businesses would still need to be successful in order to pay their monthly rents. He recognized, however, that some might argue a landlord deserves a bigger share of the profit—that it's unfair to make a landlord wait through a 10-year lease before raising rents.

"Maybe it's not 10 years. Maybe it's five years," says El-Najjar. "These are the kind of pushbacks that would be amazing to get at a public hearing where people can bring up these things."

A Standard Practice in the United Kingdom

While legislation akin to SBJSA may not exist in any other part of the United States, something quite similar exists in the United Kingdom. The Landlord and Tenant Act of 1954 established the right of tenants to renew their leases—what the English call "security of tenure"—with landlords able to regain their property in certain circumstances. As in SBJSA, a landlord and tenant can agree on the rent in their new lease or turn to an arbitrator or court to set a new rent.

There are three differences between the UK's policy and SBJSA, and the first two might make the UK's policy more flexible for landlords.

First, the British law allows landlords and tenants to agree on a contract in which the tenant signs away their right to lease renewal. For instance, property owners of highly desired spaces in popular shopping centers might only take on tenants who agree to give away their right to lease renewal. Second, there is no required length of the lease. Third, when the court decides on a new rent, it looks only at one factor, not a dozen: the comparable market rents in the surrounding area. This could be a disadvantage to the landlord, whose operating costs and mortgage costs would not be taken into account.

Tom Entwistle, a writer and landlord in the United Kingdom who provides advice to property owners through his site LandlordZONE, said that the law is widely accepted in England.

"I'm pretty sure at the time of introduction there would have been a big outcry from landlords but now it's accepted as normal practice," Entwistle wrote in an e-mail to City Limits. "Personally I'm against regulation whenever possible but in England both commercial and residential regulation is relatively light and gives a good balance in protecting both landlord and tenant."

Responding to American concerns about the potential negative impacts of the bill, Entwistle said he didn't see a risk of the policy discouraging business development because businesses will usually invest more in their improvement, not less, when they have stability. In addition, he said ultimately "who operates where in big cities comes down to economic forces" but that the bill does help protect small mom-and-pop stores that have "built up a valuable business over years in a locale and would suffer greatly if moved on."

England is no socialist country, but their embrace of "security of tenure" is certainly a step that the United States has yet to make. Constitutional questions aside, the political hurtles to SBJSA passage seem nearly insurmountable. It's not just that supporters would have to fight and win a battle with landlords big and small. It's that advocates would need to change a lot of minds about what makes a healthy economy.

"That's a pretty big step for New York City," says James Parrott, an economist at the Fiscal Policy Institute who says he has no position on the bill. "The real-estate lobby and the city would see that as an enormous incursion as a right to charge what they feel the market can bear."

> *"Time and time again, urban green spaces have been shown to improve public health outcomes, protect water quality, and decrease violence."*

Urban Green Space Projects Are Revitalizing US Cities

Joanna Parkman

In the following viewpoint, Joanna Parkman makes the case that urban improvement projects like parks and other green spaces can benefit everyone in the neighborhood. The author presents six examples of urban green space projects and the effects they have had on their cities. Introducing new and improved green spaces, such as parks, to an urban neighborhood is shown to have both positive and negative effects. Green spaces are good for public health and may decrease violence. But they can also invite gentrification into a neighborhood by making it more attractive. Parkman writes about the environment and human rights.

As you read, consider the following questions:

1. What are the positive effects of green spaces?
2. How can green space creation actually be a bad thing?
3. Overall, does the author present green spaces in cities as a positive or a negative thing?

"6 Urban Green Space Projects That Are Revitalizing U.S. Cities," by Joanna Parkman, Care2.com, Inc., January 24, 2016. Reprinted by permission.

C ity living can be a major obstacle to enjoying the outdoors, but urban designers and civic planners are pushing to change that. Say hello to innovative and sustainable mixed-use urban green space projects. Or you could just call them parks.

What makes a few acres of grass a worthy investment? Time and time again, urban green spaces have been shown to improve public health outcomes, protect water quality, and decrease violence. Parks can also alleviate some of the emotional symptoms of urban life, including stress and anxiety.

Children, in particular, can reap huge benefits from an open place safe for play and exploration. One recent study points to improvements in attention and memory for young students with more green space around their schools. And some pediatricians are opting to hand out "park prescriptions" for overweight or obese patients.

Furthermore, public green spaces can revive abandoned parts of the city, converting brownfields, vacant lots and former industrial sites into vibrant areas for community activities, ranging from free symphonies to good old pick-up soccer games.

Unfortunately, green spaces don't always bring about positive change. With more aesthetically pleasing urban landscapes comes inevitable gentrification. This usually takes the form of higher property values driving out longtime residents and disproportionately impacting low income populations and people of color. Neighborhoods with community gardens are a prime example.

But that's not to say we shouldn't continue to implement green space projects. One strategy to combat this sort of resident turnover lies in making neighborhoods "just green enough" to reap the benefits, while still deterring greedy developers. Regardless of scope, green space projects should strive to take a participatory approach that accounts for a diversity of stakeholders. Genuine local involvement remains the key to longterm positive impact.

Here are several standout examples of green space successes:

Atlanta BeltLine

The Atlanta BeltLine has gone from master's thesis to tourist attraction in an impressive span of just 17 years. The greenway inhabits an old railroad corridor encircling the city's downtown and connects 45 neighborhoods and a number of parks. Most notably, the BeltLine boasts an affordable housing program to protect vulnerable residents from displacement. Free exercise classes, a lantern parade, and an arboretum are just a sampling of the BeltLine's many attractions. And you certainly can't miss the abundant murals and street art courtesy of projects like Living Walls and Tiny Doors ATL.

Brooklyn Bridge Park

Brooklyn Bridge Park is quite the sight. 85 acres of waterfront property offer breathtaking views of Manhattan that you can enjoy while playing volleyball or fishing. Bocce and the infamous carousel add to the park's charm. Oh, and there's free public kayaking too. On the educational side of things, the Brooklyn Bridge Park Conservancy operates an Environmental Education Center that reaches more than 10,000 students each year. Children can get a firsthand look at local ecology with the Center's seining program.

Railroad Park

Railroad Park graces Birmingham, Alabama's downtown with its 19 acres of green space. The park distinguishes itself by integrating the industrial history of the city while featuring sustainable design elements like a bio-filtration wetlands area. Over 600 trees, three skate bowls, and the Birmingham History Wall also coexist here. Camille Spratling, the park's executive director, notes that Railroad Park acts as a unifier, "a place where people of all walks of life in the city come together." And with Birmingham's rich legacy of civil rights activism, that might just be its best feature.

Klyde Warren Park

Klyde Warren Park is one of the more imaginative green spaces out there. The park was constructed as a five acre deck over an eight lane highway. Klyde Warren helps connect downtown Dallas by allowing for pedestrian and bicycle traffic between Uptown and the Dallas Arts District. Dallas' city parks manager John Reynolds reports that Klyde Warren has transformed the surrounding urban environment: "Being out there now, it has changed from an inhospitable, no-man's land to a pretty comfortable space. It was almost overwhelming how much noise and traffic was there. It's a lot calmer than I ever anticipated."

Millenium Park

Millennium Park might be most well-known for "the bean," an irresistibly shiny sculpture actually entitled Cloud Gate. But details aside, Chicago's world-class public park is impressive for a number of reasons. The park, designed in part by legendary architect Frank Gehry, used to be an untouchable industrial wasteland. Now it's anything but with a five acre perennial garden and a state-of-the-art concert venue. The Boeing Galleries offer outdoor viewing of public art exhibitions, ensuring that art is accessible to everyone. Beyond that, Millennium Park boasts the title of world's largest green roof—24.5 acres of it!

The Highline (and the Lowline?)

Nowadays a trip to New York City seems to be synonymous with a visit to The High Line. The park inhabits a preserved railway formerly threatened by demolition. Garden designer Piet Oudolf found inspiration in the wild vegetation springing up from the abandoned train tracks and let this tiny bit of urban wilderness dictate the style of future plantings. That means native and low maintenance varieties make up most of what you'll encounter. The High Line itself functions as a green roof with both plants and porous pathways absorbing water and limiting stormwater runoff. Drip irrigation, integrated pest management and composting demonstrate the park's commitment to sustainability. And it wouldn't be New York without an ample supply of art.

You may not know about the High Line's future sibling, the Lowline. The plan is to take over the former Williamsburg Bridge Trolley Terminal and use cutting edge solar technology to create an underground green space. The Lowline would be the world's first underground park. And now there are murmurs that a "Green Line" will run along Broadway. Props to NYC for getting behind urban parks.

*"Focusing on improving
environmental issues helps
communities with everything
from public health to education
and economics."*

Green Spaces Come at a Price That Not Everyone Can Afford

Brentin Mock

*In the following viewpoint, Brentin Mock argues that, while
introducing green spaces and other environmental improvements
to low-income neighborhoods seems like a noble endeavor, often
these improvements drive up rents and other amenities to the
extent that residents can no longer afford to live in the community.
The author wonders whether projects intended to improve
neighborhoods' natural environments can be successful without
also inviting gentrification. He explores projects where existing
neighborhoods received environmental improvements and where
those neighborhoods stand once the projects are completed. Mock
is justice editor for* Grist *magazine.*

"Can We Green the Hood Without Gentrifying It?" by Brentin Mock, *Grist Magazine, Inc.*,
February 9, 2015. Reprinted by permission.

As you read, consider the following questions:

1. What is meant by the term "environmental gentrification"?
2. What are some of the reasons why these projects weren't as successful as designers hoped?
3. How has racism affected some environmental projects in the past?

N ow that we have established that gentrification is a thing, at least for those impacted by it, it's worth noting that there are good and bad sides to it, and that includes when neighborhoods get environmental makeovers.

Neighborhood improvements like upgraded sewage infrastructure, LEED-certified green buildings, and bike lanes are great, but, counterintuitively, they can freak out residents of under-resourced communities who fear that such projects might price them out. When that happens, you've got what Jennifer Wolch, a professor at the University of California, Berkeley, calls "environmental gentrification."

The National Environmental Justice Advisory Council (NEJAC), a committee of non-government, community-based stakeholders that helps steer EPA policies, examined this phenom in its 2006 report, "The Unintended Impacts of Redevelopment and Revitalization Efforts in Five Environmental Justice Communities." A key passage from that report:

> [F]rom the perspective of gentrified and otherwise displaced residents and small businesses, it appears that the revitalization of their cities is being built on the back of the very citizens who suffered, in-place, through the times of abandonment and disinvestment. While these citizens are anxious to see their neighborhoods revitalized, they want to be able to continue living in their neighborhoods and participate in that revitalization.

D.C. was one of the five environmental justice communities studied for the report, with a focus on Navy Yard, the southeastern neighborhood that sits along the Anacostia river. Today, nine years after that report, the Navy Yard has been almost completely transformed from its former less-than-welcoming conditions. Once saturated with the blighted brown-space of abandoned federal buildings, it's now flush with greenspace, bike lanes, a gorgeous set of condos, apartments, and townhouses overlooking the river. You won't find anyone of any race who would argue that Navy Yard is a worse off place than what it was before, but the process of getting to this point was messy, according to the NEJAC report:

> While outreach activities and Navy leadership were noteworthy, these programs achieved lower than expected success rates. This dynamic was mostly due to the community being unprepared to leverage opportunities and the government's inability to provide greater assistance due to bureaucratic atrophy and entrenchment among federal and local agencies, turf issues, and personalities. Additionally, local nonprofits lacked the necessary capacity to take advantage of the revitalization process.

Today, African Americans living in the mostly working-class and low-income Anacostia neighborhood no doubt have Navy Yard, as well as super-gentrified D.C. communities like Columbia Heights, on their minds as they hear about new plans to restore the longtime, pollution-plagued Anacostia river. Many in the Anacostia community have wondered for years if new riverfront developments on their side will mean turning the neighborhood into an unaffordable, condo-palooza like the one staring them in the face right across the river.

Those anxieties are understandable, considering that D.C. is one of the fastest gentrifying cities in the nation. According to *Governing* magazine's analysis of 2009–2013 American Community Survey data and the US2010 Longitudinal Tract Data Base, less than 5 percent of D.C. neighborhoods that consisted of mostly low-income households were gentrified between 1990 and 2000. Since then, close to 52 percent of predominantly low-income neighborhoods have gentrified.

I discussed these residential anxieties with Doug Siglin, executive director of the Anacostia River Initiative, which has

INVADING A COMMUNITY

It isn't fun when you have to leave home because you cannot afford it anymore. The moment you stop recognizing the people around you always makes the place you call "home" feel unfamiliar.

Things started to take a turn. I became aware of an "invasion" after watching a video in junior high of a white woman who disguised her voice, but video recorded my neighborhood asking other white people to take advantage of the "stupid" residents and the cheap rent. Not too long after, I noticed the houses that looked run down for years, but still had faithful inhabitants, began to go under repair. There was more effort for our neighborhood to seem appealing. More white people moved across the street. My friends moved away one by one. Condominiums were quickly built. We became neighbors with coffee shops and art galleries. More murals went up.

When community stores close and change into art galleries, that's when you know you've lost—for real. Things only got "better" when more white people decided to move into Bushwick, Brooklyn. No one really cared about us here before. We just dealt with it. We created a culture. We created a community among ourselves, and we were proud of it. Home stopped being home, and it took us by surprise.

People from Williamsburg, people from an area of Brooklyn that's becoming more and more gentrified, suddenly don't want to be associated with another culture while ironically attempting to "diversify" their inner-city urban experience. White gentrifiers want "Sex in the City." My culture is too much for them. Participating in a Puerto Rican community and learning the history behind the people that have always lived in the area is such a difficult task that it has to change for those who can't understand it. Gentrifiers want the authenticity of "exoticness" when it comes in a sushi roll or street cart empanada. Gentrification does not want me, personally.

Spike Lee said it best: "I mean, they just move in the neighborhood. You just can't come in the neighborhood. I'm for democracy and letting everybody live, but you gotta have some respect. You can't just come in when people have a culture that's been laid down for generations and you come in and now s--- gotta change because you're here?"

"Urban Gentrification Destroys Cultures and Communities," by Malika Giddens, *The Ithacan*, September 17, 2014.

been helping lead river cleanup initiatives. His focus is not only on the river, but also the 1,200-plus acres of land along its east bank that belongs to the federal government, but sits empty, except for a bunch of weeds and wild trees. On gentrification, Siglin said simply, "It's happening."

The bigger question, said Siglin, is its pace—will it be overwhelming or gradual? Another question he wrestles with: "What does improving that area, and what does improving the pollution of the river really have to do with the dynamic of people beginning to move across the river and how the communities [start] changing?"

To make sure that community members truly do have ownership and leadership in the planning, Siglin has partnered with people like Dennis Chestnut of Anacostia Groundwork, which has been organizing around this since 2007. "What we'd like to be able to do is help to sequence and control that movement so it isn't overwhelming to the people who live there," said Siglin.

He's also allied with former D.C. mayor Anthony Williams, who heads Federal City Council, a nonprofit that's been at the forefront of D.C. improvement initiatives since 1954. Williams' administration is credited (or blamed, depending on who you talk to) with spurring the massive revitalization and gentrification seen throughout D.C. over the past decade. The question on many people's minds is what's in store for Anacostia once the river is improved?

"The original idea was to focus on an idea that would bring the city together, across racial and ethnic, income and even regional lines," said Williams when I spoke to him in December about the Anacostia initiative. "A project that would embrace the environment is key to the future of the city, right? And the Anacostia is one of the most polluted rivers, if not the most polluted river in the country, and it's within blocks of the capitol. So it's important to address the environment … and, to use a hackneyed term, be sustainable."

Focusing on improving environmental issues helps communities with everything from public health to education and economics, said Williams, and so he sees the project as "the answer to pretty much every question."

D.C. has used environmental restoration to answer questions like these before, though. In the early 1920s, Congress appropriated hundreds of thousands of dollars to cleanse areas along the Potomac River and the Tidal Basin (near where the national monuments stand today) to create beaches and parks for tourists and residents. In Andrew Kahrl's book *The Land Was Ours*, he writes that the newly designed waterfront was produced with an "emphasis on unified, orderly urban spaces conducive to a healthy social order, and its faith in the ability to enhance public health, and thereby reshape society, through improving the environmental conditions of the city."

But the district did not consider African Americans in those plans. Clarence O. Sherrill, appointed by President Warren G. Harding as the superintendent of public buildings and grounds in 1921, set policies to ensure that black residents would not enjoy these new waterfront amenities. Instead, they were granted access to beaches and parts of the river that were heavily polluted.

"This … was the direct result of improvements made to urban shorelines for the benefit of others," wrote Kahrl.

Such intentional racial exclusion may no longer exist today, but the discriminatory outcomes of urban improvement persist in D.C. NEJAC's 2006 report tells how "EPA may have unintentionally exacerbated historical gentrification and dis-placement," through its brownfield remediation and watershed cleanup efforts. This has been true of both the public and private sectors.

It may explain, in part, why companies and nonprofits hoping to implant new environmentally friendly goods and services in neighborhoods of color are often met with suspicion. I started a series last year about how solar companies have been meeting resistance from some African American organizations and elected officials. As reported today in the *L.A. Times*, solar companies are baffled that anyone wouldn't want all this sunny, delightful electricity they want to bring to poor, black neighborhoods. It's not that black communities don't want it, but rather that they're painfully aware of the price tag—not what it might cost them in bills, but what it has cost them historically.

Anyone looking to correct that history should read the NEJAC report, which provides six recommendations for how to prevent outcomes like what happened with the Navy Yard. Among them are making sure "all stakeholders should have the opportunity for meaningful involvement in redevelopment and revitalization projects," and encouraging "an initial neighborhood demographic assessment and a projected impact assessment regarding displacement at the earliest possible time in a redevelopment or revitalization project."

The EPA, which was the target of the report, responded kindly to the recommendations, calling them "valuable and insightful." The agency pledged to take stronger leadership and oversight in coordinating public outreach efforts, and made community involvement a requirement in ranking criteria for brownfield cleanup grant applications. The agency also said it would consider initiating demographic analyses "where and when appropriate" in efforts to curtail displacement. EPA's correspondent on this was the Office of Solid Waste and Emergency Response, an office that environmental justice advocates often credit with producing adequate models for equity analyses.

Measures like these have also been adopted by proponents of "equitable development," a growth model pushed lately by urban planners who say that it can usher in neighborhood improvement without displacing longtime residents. The private sector might do well to follow the same playbook.

| *"Cities are the place to be these days, which means big changes for the historic communities that have populated urban cores."*

Urban Revitalization Doesn't Have to Lead to Gentrification

Jared Green

In the following viewpoint, Jared Green addresses a clear question: Can an urban neighborhood or area be revitalized without inevitably causing gentrification? Using the city of Washington, DC, as an example, the author shows how city demographics have changed because of urban revitalization. He also examines plans for new projects and the possible repercussions of those projects. Involving residents in plans from the beginning is the key to ensuring a solution for everyone. Green is editor and writer of The Dirt, *a publication of the American Society of Landscape Architects.*

As you read, consider the following questions:

1. What statistics does the author present about demographic shifts in revitalized areas?
2. What would be a "balanced" solution to urban renewal?
3. What is seen as being the best way to create revitalization without gentrification?

C ities are the place to be these days, which means big changes for the historic communities that have populated urban cores. While much of the urban renewal experiments of the 1940s through the 1960s have been deemed disasters, word is still out on the new wave of "urban revitalization" that began in the 1990s and continues through to today in most of America's cities. The supporters of revitalization say rising tides lift all boats. As wealth has come back to cities, everyone benefits. But critics of revitalization simply call it gentrification, and, as one speaker at the EcoDistricts Summit in Washington, D.C. said, "gentrification is a crime." Furthermore, new discussions of turning existing urban neighborhoods into "ecodistricts" may just be gentrification in a green dress. How can cities encourage growth but also provide a sense of continuity? How can over-taxed city planning departments accommodate the forces of change while also respecting local communities and cultures?

According to Charles Hostovsky, a professor of urban planning at Catholic University in Washington, D.C., the speed of revitalization in D.C. has been extraordinarily rapid. Every neighborhood has cranes, signifying new development. There has been a corresponding shift in the demographics of the city. In 1970, the city was 77 percent African American. Today, it's just 49 percent. "The number of people who have been displaced equals a small town." Indeed: in the past decade, approximately 50,000 young, white Millennials have moved into the city while 35,000 African Americans have left.

Reyna Alorro, who works for the DC Office of the Deputy Mayor for Planning, said revitalization has even spread east of the Anacostia River, perhaps the last hold out to gentrification. There, the city is supporting the redevelopment of Barry Farm, 25 acres of public housing, into a new mixed-income, mixed-use development that they hope will be an example of equitable revitalization. As HUD Hope IV funds have diminished since 2005, the District has started its own program of revamping public housing. "We want to target the areas with blight, crime, high unemployment and turn them into mixed income communities." The theory is that reducing the concentration of the poor in communities, and relieving their isolation, will improve their conditions.

Barry Farm, a historic African American community founded by freed slaves, currently has some 400 units, with 1,200 people. The population of the housing development is 93 percent single mothers; some 86 percent are unemployed. "This is not a friendly, welcoming site." There is only one over-priced corner store, with a bullet-proof glass wall separating the store owners from customers.

The $550 million redevelopment plan, said Kelly Smyser, DC Housing Authority, will create 1,400 public and affordable apartments at the same site. New apartments will face each other, creating open public thoroughfares that enable "eyes on the street." There will also be a recreation center, with an indoor pool, basketball courts, and computer labs, as well as a charter school. The nearby Anacostia Metro station will get a full upgrade, with improved access to the station from the development. "We want to bring opportunity to residents. We will make the connection to Metro easier and safer."

The District government calls this project "revitalization without gentrification," as all current residents will be allowed to come back to the new development. "There will be zero displacement." The city also promises it will undertake a program of "build first before demolition." To increase the diversity of the development, some 300 of the new units will be affordable housing, rentals, or for sale. The city also wants to encourage small businesses to locate in Barry Farms. They are creating "live-work" sites that will enable people to live above their stores. "We need to get rid of the bullet proof glass."

The neighborhood is rightly concerned about how they can preserve the best of the local culture with all the change. One example of this is the Goodman League, a basketball tournament that happens in the neighborhood every year. "People have a good time, barbequing, sitting in lawn chairs. There are no

WHY PRESERVE THE PAST?

Historic preservation activists have long struggled against the field's negative reputation. Some critics say it's an avenue for gentrification, only focuses on preserving a narrow, elitist slice of history (i.e. that of those who are wealthy, white and male), or is simply a nostalgic grasp on the past that does not allow for needed growth and revitalization.

In her new book, *The Past and Future City: How Historic Preservation Is Reviving America's Communities*, Stephanie Meeks dives into those perceptions in an attempt to prove historic preservation is one of the most important urbanist movements of the time. Meeks is president and CEO of the National Trust for Historic Preservation, which last week released its annual list of endangered "landmarks." Ultimately, Meeks argues, historic preservation is both a way to save beautiful old buildings and the stories they carry, and to deeply engage with the local community and their concerns and needs.

On redefining what historic preservation is:

"We do not honor the historic buildings in our midst, nor those who once inhabited them, by trapping these structures in amber or sequestering them away behind velvet ropes. We do it by working to see that they continue to play a vibrant role at the heart of the community."

beefs on the court." The basketball courts where this happen will remain untouched.

While Smyser was convinced this upgrade will benefit the community, one conference attendee seemed equally as convinced that with the District's multimillion dollar investment, the city will simply be opening the neighborhood to opportunistic developers and further gentrification. Word is still out on how this urban redevelopment story will play out.

Hazel Edwards, a professor of planning at Catholic University, outlined some examples of successful revitalization without gentrification in other parts of the US. She pointed to Melrose

On inclusive preservation:

"Preservation is about ensuring that our urban landscape reflects more than just profit margins or the whims of developers and real estate speculators—that they address the real needs and concerns of communities. It is about working to see that we honor and reflect the full contours of our past, including the complex and difficult chapters."

On preventing displacement:

"The job of historic preservation is not to try to prevent change—communities are always in the process of change. Rather is it to leverage the tools, techniques and habits of our field to help neighborhoods move forward in a positive direction, in a way that minimized community disruption and helps facilitate equity, affordability and harmony among old residents and new arrivals."

"... [H]istoric preservation can no longer just be about saving old places, independent of the men, women and children who live among them. We have to see that diverse history is being honored and diverse stories are being told. And we need to see that the concerns of families are heard, and their needs met, by adaptive reuse projects and urban revitalization strategies."

**"High-Profile Historic Preservationist Makes the Case for Saving Buildings,"
by Kelsey E. Thomas, Next City, October 12, 2016.**

Commons in South Bronx, where a group of local residents banded together in the early 1990s into a group called Nos Quedamos (We Stay) and fought back New York City government's imposed urban renewal plan. With the help of an altruistic architect, Nos Quedamos forged their own urban design that respected the community's unique cultural heritage. The plan and design resulted in 2,000 units of affordable housing. "There was no displacement in the community."

In Portland, Oregon, Edwards told us about a project called Cully Main Street plan, which helped preserve one the most diverse neighborhoods in Portland, with some 40–50 percent people of color. They devised a plan to equitably bring in commercial activity to their main street while accommodating an influx of new white homeowners and preserving the neighborhood diversity.

Edwards said the key to revitalization without gentrification is "bringing residents and the community to the table often and at the beginning." This kind of public planning process requires a great investment of time and resources by city governments, but without this investment, the only result may be inequitable, developer-led urban revitalization. "Cities have to form diverse, inclusive partnerships, foster openness, and collaborate on goals and outcomes."

Quoting the urban leader and author, Kaid Benfield, she said, "we have to work towards a balanced solution," and also track our progress to see whether we are living up to our goals.

Periodical and Internet Sources Bibliography

The following articles have been selected to supplement the diverse views presented in this chapter.

John Buntin, "The Myth of Gentrification," *Slate*, January 14, 2015. http://www.slate.com/articles/news_and_politics/politics /2015/01/the_gentrification_myth_it_s_rare_and_not_as_bad _for_the_poor_as_people.html.

Michelle Chen, "Can Neighborhoods Be Revitalized Without Gentrifying Them?," *Nation*, April 11, 2016. https://www .thenation.com/article/trusting-baltimore-communities/.

Richard Florida, "The Closest Look Yet at Gentrification and Displacement," *CityLab*, November 2, 2015. https://www.citylab .com/equity/2015/11/the-closest-look-yet-at-gentrification-and -displacement/413356/.

Juliet Kahne, "Does Placemaking Cause Gentrification? It's Complicated," Project for Public Spaces, November 2, 2015. https://www.pps.org/article/gentrification.

Ed Leefeldt, "Where Gentrification Is Having the Biggest Impact on Cities," CBS MoneyWatch, March 5, 2018. https://www.cbsnews .com/news/does-gentrification-help-or-hurt-our-major-cities/.

Deandrea Salvador, "Can Curbing Gentrification Help Stop Climate Change?," *Pacific Standard*, January 25, 2016. https://psmag.com /news/can-curbing-gentrification-help-stop-climate-change.

Michael Sliwinski, "Gentrification: What Is It Doing to Our Urban Centers?," Law Street Media, October 6, 2015. https:// lawstreetmedia.com/issues/business-and-economics /gentrification-transforming-urban-centers-isnt/.

Susie Smith, "Environmental Gentrification," Critical Sustainabilities. Retrieved April 28, 2018. https://critical-sustainabilities.ucsc.edu /environmental-gentrification/.

World Bank, "Managing the Potential Undesirable Impacts of Urban Regeneration: Gentrification and Loss of Social Capital." Retrieved April 28, 2018. https://urban-regeneration.worldbank.org/node/45.

CHAPTER 2

Does Gentrification Contribute to the Housing Crisis?

Chapter Preface

C ity neighborhoods are communities unto themselves. A neighborhood functions with people of all different ages and economic circumstances, living together in these different types of housing. However, there may be a finite amount of housing available in a neighborhood, especially for people in lower socioeconomic groups. And two things can occur when a neighborhood begins to gentrify and becomes a place where other people want to live. First, as a neighborhood becomes more desirable, landlords often find that they can raise the rents. Renovating older apartments and apartment buildings may also bring higher rents. Second, once people start flocking to a hot neighborhood, the amount of housing available is reduced. This can especially cripple people who are forced to leave their existing residence because of increased rents.

According to the US Census Bureau, the number of vacant rental properties is now at an all-time low, but while rents are rising, most incomes are not. Evictions are also at a high rate, especially for low-income renters. These people are displaced, meaning that they often must leave their neighborhoods entirely and move to a different part of the city in order to find housing that they can afford. There is a growing gap in many cities between what people can afford to pay for housing and what housing is available in that price range. And because of the mortgage crisis that took place in 2008 and more stringent rules for the amount of credit and income needed to obtain a mortgage to purchase a house, people who once would have bought a residence are now thrust into an already overcrowded rental market.

Gentrification may be adding to an already difficult housing market for renters. Some experts argue that it actually creates richer, more diverse neighborhoods and invites redevelopment that includes low-income housing. Others believe that in a housing climate that is already approaching a crisis point for many people, gentrification is just making things worse.

"When we choose to invest in housing and transportation as economic development we will go from good to great."

Gentrification Squeezes Out People Who Make a City Run

Victoria Livingstone

In the following viewpoint, Victoria Livingstone argues that gentrification spurs an affordable living crisis. The author presents a case study of the city of Greenville, South Carolina, which is rapidly gentrifying, to make her point that a surge in popularity means that it is losing rental units that people in the lower- and middle-income brackets can afford—particularly African Americans, but also the community's schoolteachers, firefighters, and nurses. While the city has begun to set aside funds for more affordable housing, more will be needed. Livingstone is is a visiting assistant professor of Spanish at Moravian College.

"VOICES: Tackling the Affordable-Housing Crisis in a Gentrifying Southern City," by Victoria Livingstone, The Institute for Southern Studies, August 10, 2017. https://www. facingsouth.org/2017/08/voices-tackling-affordable-housing-crisis-gentrifying-southern-city. Licensed under CC BY ND 3.0.

As you read, consider the following questions:

1. What are some of the factors that led to the gentrification of Greenville?
2. Other than housing, how does gentrification negatively affect the city?
3. What are some of the possible actions that the city can take to address the housing shortage?

According to 2016 census data, 10 of the top 15 fastest-growing US cities are in the South. Number four on that list is Greenville, South Carolina. Like a number of Southern cities from Charleston to New Orleans, Greenville is rapidly becoming gentrified as the downtown area, once accessible to the working class, is becoming prohibitively expensive for residents in low- and middle-income brackets.

Greenville's revitalized downtown, which includes the picturesque Falls Park, a bike trail, concert venues, and upscale restaurants, has been featured in a number of national publications. A *New York Times* journalist recently wrote that Greenville "may be the next major food destination," and *U.S. News* named it one of the 100 best places to live in the country. Yet Greenville's growth may prove unsustainable if the negative effects of gentrification are not addressed.

According to a report submitted by a volunteer steering committee last September, Greenville now faces a shortage of 2,500 affordable housing units, despite having a surplus of low-cost housing as recently as 2000. Prices for rentals near downtown have soared, and expensive new condo complexes are being built. At the same time, older, more affordable rental properties are disappearing. According to Bucky Tarleton, a real estate advisor who has lived in Greenville since 1986, owners who once rented out their houses to working-class families for as little as $400 a month now prefer to sell for much greater profits.

"The loss of rental units is happening quietly," Tarleton said, adding that the process has the potential to "wreak havoc."

Whereas a larger city may be able to better absorb the loss of affordable rentals, Tarleton noted that the effects of gentrification may be magnified in Greenville, a city of just 65,000. Greenville residents are being pushed out of the city and into distant communities with no supermarkets, no hospitals, and limited employment opportunities.

The changes have negatively impacted the African-American community in particular. Between 2000 and 2010, Greenville's African-American population decreased by 8 percent while the white population grew, particularly in the downtown area. According to local activist Susan McLarty, the concentration of African-American students at Stone Academy, a high-performing magnet school in the downtown area, dropped from 22 percent to 16 percent between 2010 and 2016. At the same time, schools serving more diverse populations, such as Mauldin Elementary in nearby Simpsonville, are struggling. The number of students qualifying for free or reduced lunch at Mauldin jumped from 47 percent to 50 percent in the last two school years.

Of all regions of the US, the South already ranks lowest in measures of upward mobility. In Greenville, a child whose family is in the bottom fifth of household income stands only a 4.9 percent chance of rising to the top fifth, a statistic that situates Greenville County among the worst in the nation for economic mobility. Greenville must address its shortage of affordable housing in order to avoid deepening economic divisions in a region already marked by inequality.

Gentrification also presents a barrier to the growth of Greenville's service industry, which is concentrated downtown. American Grocery Restaurant, an upscale restaurant that had been in downtown Greenville for 10 years, closed last month. Stating their reasons for shutting down the business, owners Joe Clarke and Darlene Mann-Clarke mentioned the "rising rents in the city, rising food prices and the staffing challenges that restaurants are feeling nationwide."

Carl Sobocinski, president of Table 301, a restaurant group that runs eight local restaurants and employs nearly 500 people, estimates that at least 80 percent of his employees live more than five miles from downtown. Since the city lacks a reliable system of public transportation, workers who do not own cars must either spend hours waiting for infrequent buses or leave their jobs. Table 301 has begun brainstorming strategies for creating more affordable housing and is looking into the possibility of subsidizing housing for employees.

Besides workers in the restaurant industry, firefighters, health care workers, educators, and others in middle-income brackets struggle to pay rent in downtown Greenville. When these workers are pushed out of the city, other residents may find themselves affected in deeply personal ways. For example, when Grier Mullins went to visit her mother in an assisted living facility in downtown Greenville, she found the home short of caretakers and discovered that a favorite nursing assistant had left, forced out of the city by rising rents.

Local activists are playing an important role in addressing the negative effects of gentrification in Greenville. Ansel Sanders, president and CEO of the nonprofit Public Education Partners of Greenville County, is exploring creating a residential campus for public school teachers in the city. Modeled partly on the Williams-Baldwin Teacher Campus in Asheville, North Carolina, Sanders' project would offer teachers housing at below-market rates.

"There is pain in two markets," said Sanders, "a shortage of teachers and a lack of affordable housing." He sees the teacher campus as a way of addressing both problems while also sending a positive message regarding how much the community values educators.

The city has begun to respond. As a result of the steering committee's report, the city council unanimously voted to appropriate $2 million to make more affordable housing available.

But those funds are not sufficient, according to McLarty, who participated in the steering committee. She says Greenville actually needs $10 million a year over the next 20 years to catch up. But she remains hopeful.

"When we choose to invest in housing and transportation as economic development we will go from good to great," McLarty said. "Moving from our historical settlement patterns of concentrated poverty to economic integration is the key to Greenville's continued growth and vitality."

> *"Most of the more recent and more rigorous studies of gentrification find that, actually, poor residents and poor households—especially renters—do not move out of gentrifying neighborhoods at unusually high rates."*

Low-Income Renters Aren't Moving Out of Gentrifying Neighborhoods

Jarrett Murphy

In the following viewpoint, Jarrett Murphy argues that low-income families do not move out of gentrifying neighborhoods at greater rates than they move away from less gentrifying areas. The author cites studies that clash with the common perception that a neighborhood's low-income residents are forced out when white, educated, high-income residents move in. However, the author does note that in these neighborhoods, when low-income renters move out, their housing is more likely to be taken over by higher-income people moving into the neighborhood. Murphy is the executive editor and publisher of City Limits.

"The Complicated Research on How Gentrification Affects the Poor," by Jarrett Murphy, City Limits, November 20, 2015. Reprinted by permission.

As you read, consider the following questions:

1. What point is made about low-income renters and housing instability in general?
2. What kinds of statistics does the author use to argue the point in the viewpoint?
3. What are some of the possible side effects to a neighborhood when *displacement* becomes *replacement*?

F acing a rebellion by community boards across the city against zoning proposals that are crucial to the administration's affordable housing plan, Mayor de Blasio's housing chief last week argued that—contrary to conventional wisdom—gentrification does not displace low-income New Yorkers.

"Most of the more recent and more rigorous studies of gentrification find that, actually, poor residents and poor households— especially renters—do not move out of gentrifying neighborhoods at unusually high rates," Commissioner of Housing Preservation and Development Vicki Been said in a speech at the New York Law School.

Noting that low-income families typically have a high rate of housing instability even without gentrification, Been added: "Most of the research show that renters move away no more often and in many cases less often in gentrifying than in less gentrifying neighborhoods."

Been based that claim on at least five articles published over the past 11 years.

The first, a 2004 paper by Lance Freeman and Frank Braconi, looked at gentrification in New York City from 1991 to 1999, focusing on Chelsea, Harlem, the Lower East Side, Morningside Heights, Fort Greene, Park Slope and Williamsburg. Each of those neighborhoods had a higher proportion of white people, higher average rents, higher average incomes and higher educational attainment at the end of the study period. Compared to other neighborhoods of the city, however, low-income people in those gentrifying areas were 19 percent less likely to move. In

2005, Freeman wrote about the topic again, using national data. This time, he didn't find lower mobility in gentrifying areas: Instead, he found a modest increase in displacement in those neighborhoods, but it wasn't any higher for poor people.

A 2010 paper by Ingrid Gould Ellen and Katherine M. O'Regan, two researchers at the Furman Center, which Been led at the time, produced perhaps the most sanguine results:

> ... [T]he picture our analyses paint of gentrification is one in which original residents are much less harmed than is typically assumed. They do not appear to be displaced in the course of change; they experience modest gains in income during the process, and they are more satisfied with their neighborhoods in the wake of the change.

That paper, which used Census data and examined neighborhood changes in the 1990s, also found no evidence that neighborhoods that experienced a gain in income relative to the metro area as a whole saw an increase in the percentage of residents who were white. "Of course, each of these findings is based on averages; some individual neighborhoods naturally followed a different course," the researchers noted.

Indeed, these empirical studies clash directly with what seems to the naked eye to be true in some of those very neighborhoods Freeman and Braconi examined 11 years ago. How is it those communities have changed so visibly if the evidence suggests the process at play there does not typically uproot poor people?

In his 2005 work, Freeman makes an important point: What was significant in the data he studied was not so much who was or wasn't being driven *out* of gentrifying neighborhoods but who was coming *in*: people more likely to be white and with higher incomes than the original residents. Other research indicates that, as one might expect, poor people are less able to move *into* gentrifying areas than other neighborhoods. And a study of gentrification in England and Wales by Freeman, Adele Cassola and Tiacheng Cai that was published this year noted that low-income households have much higher turnover rates than other households.

GENTRIFICATION MAY HELP THE POOR

Creating enough affordable housing is one of the hardest political and economic challenges in the world. The *Washington Post* today picks up a nonpartisan California government study that looks specifically at what happens to low income people when you build more housing for high income people in their neighborhood. It is natural to imagine after a moment's thought that this sort of gentrification—which can be seen all over Brooklyn, for example, where new luxury condos sprout on blocks that were considered poor just a few years ago—would hurt the neighborhood's low income residents. In fact, the report finds, the opposite is true.

In places facing affordable housing crises—like NYC, and like parts of California, which the report focuses on—one unavoidable fact is that there is simply not enough housing. Housing that was once affordable becomes unaffordable due to the lack of new supply to keep up with increasing demand. For this reason, the study found that one very simple way to help ease the affordable housing crisis is to allow more private construction—even if that construction is not of affordable housing.

For one, the report notes, the new luxury housing of today turns into the middle class housing of the future, as the rich chase ever newer housing stock. By building continuously we ensure a future supply. Furthermore, adding new units (even if they're not affordable) tends to cause rent to grow more slowly.

The study also found that—perhaps because of this effect of keeping rents in check—low-income areas with the most market-rate construction actually had lower displacement of citizens than low-income areas with less new construction. Which is to say that poorer people are actually less likely to be forced to move out of neighborhoods where developers are building lots of new buildings for gentrifiers than neighborhoods that are just plain poor, with little new building at all. And none of this is related to policies that require new buildings to set aside a certain (small) percentage of units for affordable housing: "market-rate housing construction appears to be associated with less displacement regardless of a community's inclusionary housing policies."

"Study: Building Luxury Housing for Gentrifiers Helps the Poor," by Hamilton Nolan, Gawker.com, February 12, 2016.

Put it all together, and you've got this: Gentrification might not drive poor people out of neighborhoods, but gentrifying neighborhoods are where there's a greater risk that when low-income households leave their apartments those spots will be taken up by wealthier people. In other words, the issue isn't *dis*placement of the poor, but *re*placement.

That's important. Population movement isn't the only thing that bothers people about gentrification. A change in the feel of the neighborhood is often at the heart of the anxiety that accompanies development: beloved businesses close, the culture of a neighborhood shifts. Ethnic succession has always been a fact of life in New York City's neighborhoods but when the change happens suddenly it's rarely welcome. Resistance to such a shift can, at times, be ugly—think of the bigotry that greeted black families moving into white neighborhoods in the 1960s—but the sentiment can also be perfectly understandable, especially when the change is seen as the result of deliberate city policy, not the city's organic evolution.

What's more, the impact of gentrification is about more than who comes, who leaves and who stays but what kind of life each group enjoys. Some of the research cited by HPD indicates that low-income people in gentrifying neighborhoods generally believe their quality of life has improved and see modest growth in their own incomes. But a low-income person who remains in a gentrifying neighborhood is likely to face higher rents and higher prices at the grocery store.

And what of those who leave? A 2015 study of gentrification in Philadelphia found that when more vulnerable residents depart gentrifying neighborhoods, "they are more likely to move to lower-income neighborhoods and neighborhoods with lower values on quality- of-life indicators." Specifically, people with low credit scores "are more likely to move to neighborhoods closer to their origin neighborhoods and neighborhoods with lower income, worse economic conditions, higher crime rates, and lower-performing public schools."

| "It just started raining and I can't say
where I will be sleeping tonight."

The Housing Crisis Is Worse Without Gentrification

Jake Blumgart

In the following excerpted viewpoint, Jake Blumgart argues that there is a housing crisis in America that has nothing to do with gentrification. The author tells the story of someone who is experiencing the housing crisis firsthand, and he illustrates the frustration felt by someone who cannot find stable and affordable housing. While the story takes place in an economically depressed city, the examples of the housing crisis and the need for affordable housing relate to many cities in the United States. Blumgart is a contributing writer at Next City *whose work also appears regularly in* Al Jazeera America, *the* Philadelphia Inquirer, *and* Pacific Standard.

As you read, consider the following questions:

1. What are some of the factors that made it difficult for Donnie Evans to find stable housing?
2. What trend is taking palace when it comes to people buying homes in the city?
3. What are some possible actions that could help Chester, Pennsylvania, provide more affordable housing?

"The Housing Crisis We Don't Talk About," by Jake Blumgart, Next City, October 20, 2014. Reprinted by permission.

D onnie Evans, an itinerant handyman in the city of Chester, Pa., desperately needed somewhere to stay.

A former dockworker who had struggled to get by since the city's shipyards closed in 1989, Evans, 51, was in a fight with his girlfriend. The one thing they agreed on was that it would be best for him to move out of the apartment they shared—and fast. The situation felt urgent; he had no leads on apartments he could afford, and the waiting lists for the Chester Housing Authority's Section 8 vouchers and project-based housing were closed. When a landlord Evans knew offered him a place, he did not refuse.

The landlord, Allan Aigeldinger Jr., who in the past had hired him for the occasional lawn mowing or house painting or, sometimes, Evans says, a quiet illegal dump job, promised a whole house for $450 a month.

The handwritten agreement Evans and Aigeldinger signed last October is a strange sort of lease. It committed Evans to paying $450 a month in rent for a home that wasn't legally habitable and couldn't be occupied despite the rent being paid—a violation of a Chester law forbidding property owners from renting property without a certificate of occupancy. The agreement stated that Evans must supply "all labor and materials" needed to restore the 74-year-old, six-room duplex to livable condition. Once those repairs were done, the agreement decreed that Aigeldinger would apply for an occupancy permit "at owner expense." Only after the application was processed and the city had issued a certificate of occupancy could Evans move into the house, a stucco twin built in 1940. The agreement included no provisions detailing the repairs needed or suggesting a timeline for the work.

Aigeldinger, who would months later admit in court he thought the agreement was favorable to Evans, took the first rent payment in cash from his not-tenant tenant, signed the agreement and issued a handwritten receipt before handing over the keys.

Though the lease said Evans wasn't to move into the place, Evans maintains the landlord knew he planned to live there. "He wrote the lease, had me sign it. I thought I was doing the right thing. I thought I had gotten a decent place to stay," Evans recalls. Aigeldinger declined to comment for this article.

As soon as he saw the place he had paid for, Evans realized his mistake. The house was really a shell of a duplex. Asbestos drooped down from one of the holes in a second-floor ceiling. Wind cut through cracks around the windows. The floor in the kitchen was completely torn up. Without the certificate of occupancy, Evans could not legally hook up running water, heat or electricity. A neighbor would periodically bring over water to flush the toilet.

Evans refused to give Aigeldinger money after his initial payment. But with nowhere else to go, he stayed in the decrepit shell through last winter, one of the coldest and snowiest in recent memory. In the bedroom, the wall turned black from the kerosene heater Evans lit to keep from freezing. Blankets were duct-taped over the windows to keep the winds at bay. He slept in a coat and gloves. It was a situation that could have turned instantly deadly.

Evans felt wronged. He never imagined he would be the one summoned to court. But in March 2014, that is exactly what happened. Aigeldinger sued Evans for $2,250 of unpaid rent and a failure to obtain a certificate of occupancy. The case was on shaky legal ground; local law in Chester forbids a property owner from collecting rent or "recover[ing] possession of the premises" without a certificate of occupancy. Evans found a lawyer through Widener University School of Law's Health, Education, and Legal Assistance Project, a non-profit civil legal aid program. When the lawyer, Jordan Mickman, called Aigeldinger, the landlord claimed Evans wasn't supposed to move in until after the repairs were complete, citing the handwritten lease both men had signed in October. He dismissed the complaints as the delusions of a drug addict. "He called me a crackhead. I don't even smoke cigarettes," recalls Evans, who opted to file a counterclaim against the landlord with the goal of retrieving his $450 plus damages, expenses he incurred working on the house and court costs.

In May, Judge Wilden Horace Davis, at the Delaware County Magisterial District Court essentially called the case a draw. Evans got $450 from Aigeldinger and was ordered to pay $185.66 in court fees, and Aigeldinger was awarded possession of the house and charged court fees of $78.93. The courts dismissed a separate case filed by the city against the landlord for renting without a certificate of occupancy.

When Evans received the $450 in mid-September, he quickly spent it on food and temporary stays in a motel. He still hasn't paid court costs and can't foresee a time when he will have the money to do so. Since leaving Aigeldinger's property in March, he has bounced around, crashing with his mother and acquaintances, and briefly reuniting with his ex-girlfriend. Mickman has tried to get him into a shelter but to be admitted, Evans needs a government-issued photo ID, which he doesn't have. When asked in late September if he would describe himself as homeless, he was quiet for a moment before responding.

"I guess you could say that," he said. "It just started raining and I can't say where I will be sleeping tonight."

No Choices

Chester was once an industrial powerhouse where ships were built, locomotives soldered and Fords assembled. All that was a long time ago and it shows. In 1998, the state built a prison on the grounds of the shuttered shipyard where Evans had worked, and before him, tens of thousands of Southern African-Americans who migrated north to build tankers during World War II. Chester's lynchpin employer, the Sun Shipbuilding and Drydocking Company, employed more blacks than any other company in America during the war but immediately shed most of these positions as the number of jobs fell from 35,000 in 1943 to 4,000 in 1947. Today, fewer people live in the entire city than worked on that waterfront in 1943. Backhoes have demolished entire neighborhoods, leaving weedy lots where Chester feels almost abandoned. The occasional loose pit bull roams around the less trafficked areas.

"I feel like I woke up one morning and everything was gone, even the houses were gone," says Vanessa Duson-Smith, a life-long resident of Chester. "Whole neighborhoods were gone. You ride down Third Street, you see nothing but empty lots, those were all neighborhoods. We played in those houses. In the last 10 years Chester has totally died, now they're just putting the dirt over it."

But if Chester is a mausoleum, it is one with almost 34,000 people living within its dilapidated walls—the majority of them—61.5 percent—paying rent to do so.

Chester is what is known, in real estate industry jargon, as a "weak market city." The phrase means what it sounds like. The city is poor and its economy stagnant. The median home sale price in Chester in 2012 was $20,000, compared to $69,350 in nearby Wilmington and $98,000 in Philadelphia. Fewer than half of Chester's working-age adults are employed, and a third of the population is living at or below the poverty line. In a city where median rent is $790, 51.5 percent of households pay 35 percent or more of their income to their landlords.

At a time when some of its peers in the region—like Wilmington and Philadelphia—are showing signs of new life, Chester remains trapped in its postindustrial doldrums. One result of this grim stasis is a severely compromised housing market.

"It's attractive for people to buy cheap properties and rent them out for as much as they can get without maintaining them, because people in Chester really don't have very much recourse," said Robert Salvin, a lawyer who used to work in the city for Community Impact Legal Services and now runs Bala Cynwyd's Philadelphia Debt Clinic and Consumer Law Center.

Aigeldinger bought the shell he rented to Evans for $20,000 in 2007, according to Delaware County records. Records indicate that he made no significant investment into the house after buying it and instead, let it sit vacant until Evans expressed an interest in moving in. A cursory search of county property records shows that he owns other inexpensive properties in Chester.

In 2012, there were 667 home sales in the city, but only 33 were purchased with a mortgage. (Investors generally finance their purchases through other means, so comparing mortgages to total sales is a reliable way to measure owner-occupancy.) Nationally about half of home sales are completed without a mortgage, but in Chester the proportion is nearer to one mortgage for every 20 sales. There are responsible landlords in town, ranging from larger actors like Penn Rose, which manages properties in seven states, to the members of Chester Netters, a network of roughly 40 landlords who often work with the housing authority and its Section 8-wielding tenants. But the city has also proven to be a magnet for incompetent and downright neglectful absentee operators.

There are so few decent landlords in Chester that Mickman tries to reserve the full weight of judgment for the very worst.

"In Chester, [the term] slumlord has to be used very selectively to maintain the value of the word," Mickman said.

Local government is no match for the market either. While many of the most desirable apartments are owned, subsidized or managed by the local housing authority, those apartments are largely spoken for. Like every other housing authority in the nation, the Chester Housing Authority is struggling to maintain its services with ever-declining support from Washington.

Outside of the housing authority, things are just as strained. With very little property tax revenue coming in to City Hall, the single city inspector charged with making sure properties meet code regulations is stretched thin. (City Councilman and Director of Public Safety William A. Jacobs did not respond to numerous requests for an interview, and messages left with the Department of Public Safety, which oversees the fire department, the building and housing division and the health department, went unanswered.)

When the inspections do happen, impact is limited.

"The inspector will issue a citation and perhaps give the tenant a civil complaint form suggesting that the tenant file a lawsuit," said Mickman. [...] The legal response would be to file a civil complaint against the landlord—with no guarantee of a win because of weak state protections for renters.

"I have never seen a Chester tenant bring a landlord to court and win, except with a lawyer, and even then [the odds are not good]," Mickman said.

[...]

Cities like Chester are, after all, the reason government got involved in the housing market in the first place. "In most cities at most times, public housing provides a better alternative than private-sector housing in poor neighborhoods," writes Edward Goetz in *New Deal Ruins: Race, Economic Justice, and Public Policy*. But federal the government long ago abandoned the idea of building more project-based public housing, and today even its cheaper alternatives, like Section 8 vouchers and low-income housing tax credits, are stunted by Congress.

The housing authority's waiting lists are likely to remain lengthy for the foreseeable future. Alan Mallach is an urban development expert who has studied Chester for the Federal Reserve Bank of Philadelphia. He expects little to change there without a major shift in direction from the state or federal government. "Unless some higher level of government is going to come in and say this is an unacceptable way for people to live, Chester is unlikely to change in any meaningful way," says Mallach. "But the federal government has, for all practical purposes, said they are out of it, good luck, when it comes to these situations. It's not a pretty picture."

> *"Beginning in the 1970s, urban life slowly began to regain prestige, particularly among artists and the highly educated."*

In Urban Areas, Change Means There Are Winners and Losers

PBS

In the following viewpoint, a companion piece to a POV *documentary called* Flag Wars, *PBS examines the changes that gentrification brings to a community, including which residents benefit and which don't. Columbus, Ohio, is an example of a city that once seemed to be in decline but has recently begun to experience a revitalization as more people decide to move back into the city from suburbs. Using Columbus as a starting point, the article clearly explains what gentrification is, what consequences it brings, and specifically, how it affects older neighborhoods and the people who live in them. PBS, the Public Broadcasting Service, produces the series* POV, *which broadcasts independent documentaries.*

"Flag Wars: What Is Gentrification?" American Documentary, Inc., June 17, 2003. Reprinted by permission.

As you read, consider the following questions:

1. What are the positive effects of gentrification? What are the negative effects?
2. How do demographics change with gentrification?
3. How does gentrification affect a neighborhood in terms of race, class, and culture?

Flag Wars tells the story of what happened to the Olde Towne East community in Columbus, Ohio when the neighborhood went through the process of gentrification in the mid-to-late 1990s. For much of the twentieth century, urbanists, policymakers, and activists were preoccupied with inner city decline across the United States, as people with money and options fled cities for the suburbs. But widespread reports of the American city's demise proved premature. Beginning in the 1970s, urban life slowly began to regain prestige, particularly among artists and the highly educated. By the turn of this century, many cities were thriving again, and their desirability among the wealthy and upwardly mobile was putting intense pressure on rents, real estate prices, and low-income communities.

What Is Gentrification?

Gentrification is a general term for the arrival of wealthier people in an existing urban district, a related increase in rents and property values, and changes in the district's character and culture. The term is often used negatively, suggesting the displacement of poor communities by rich outsiders. But the effects of gentrification are complex and contradictory, and its real impact varies.

Many aspects of the gentrification process are desirable. Who wouldn't want to see reduced crime, new investment in buildings and infrastructure, and increased economic activity in their neighborhoods? Unfortunately, the benefits of these changes are often enjoyed disproportionately by the new arrivals, while the established residents find themselves economically and socially marginalized.

Gentrification has been the cause of painful conflict in many American cities, often along racial and economic fault lines. Neighborhood change is often viewed as a miscarriage of social justice, in which wealthy, usually white, newcomers are congratulated for "improving" a neighborhood whose poor, minority residents are displaced by skyrocketing rents and economic change.

Although there is not a clear-cut technical definition of gentrification, it is characterized by several changes.

Demographics: An increase in median income, a decline in the proportion of racial minorities, and a reduction in household size, as low-income families are replaced by young singles and couples.

Real Estate Markets: Large increases in rents and home prices, increases in the number of evictions, conversion of rental units to ownership (condos) and new development of luxury housing.

Land Use: A decline in industrial uses, an increase in office or multimedia uses, the development of live-work "lofts" and high-end housing, retail, and restaurants.

Culture and Character: New ideas about what is desirable and attractive, including standards (either informal or legal) for architecture, landscaping, public behavior, noise, and nuisance.

How Does It Happen?

America's renewed interest in city life has put a premium on urban neighborhoods, few of which have been built since World War II. If people are flocking to new jobs in a region where housing is scarce, pressure builds on areas once considered undesirable.

Gentrification tends to occur in districts with particular qualities that make them desirable and ripe for change. The convenience, diversity, and vitality of urban neighborhoods are major draws, as is the availability of cheap housing, especially if the buildings are distinctive and appealing. Old houses or

RENTERS VS. OWNERS

Gentrification is the hottest of hot-button urban issues. Many activists and critics see it as essentially a process by which more affluent and educated white newcomers displace poorer, working-class black residents. But those who have studied the subject closely, like Columbia University urban planner Lance Freeman, believe that the issue of displacement is more myth than reality. In fact, Freeman's detailed empirical research has found that the probability of a family being displaced by gentrification in New York City was a mere 1.3 percent ...

The study generates three big takeaways which update and extend our understanding of gentrification and displacement.

Renters are nearly two times more likely to be displaced by gentrification than homeowners

Controlling for other factors, renters face a 2.6 percent greater probability of being displaced in a gentrifying neighborhood compared to 1.3 percent overall. While this may seem small, it's greater than the difference between residents of subsidized and unsubsidized units and about the same as the difference between a married renter and one who is divorced.

As the study notes: "If we think that divorce or the loss of a rental subsidy makes a substantial difference for the likelihood of an involuntary move, then we may say the same of gentrification."

industrial buildings often attract people looking for "fixer-uppers" as investment opportunities.

Gentrification works by accretion—gathering momentum like a snowball. Few people are willing to move into an unfamiliar neighborhood across class and racial lines. Once a few familiar faces are present, more people are willing to make the move. Word travels that an attractive neighborhood has been "discovered" and the pace of change accelerates rapidly.

Consequences of Gentrification

In certain respects, a neighborhood that is gentrified can become a "victim of its own success." The upward spiral of desirability and increasing rents and property values often erodes the very

Gentrification has virtually no effect on homeowners' moves

Why does gentrification have essentially no discernible effect on homeowners moving out of the neighborhood? Owners have more money and more equity in their homes. Their costs are locked in and do not rise like rents do. Homeowners also tend to be older and more attached to the neighborhoods they live in. Factors like jobs, schools, and community institutions keep them in the neighborhood in addition to their economic interests ...

For renters, gentrification might mean rising rent or an increased threat of eviction. For homeowners, it might mean a chance to sell a home for unexpected windfall ...

Property taxes do not increase displacement

Third, there is limited evidence that property taxes can displace homeowners. This occurs only among homeowners where property taxes eat up an extraordinarily high fraction of their incomes. The effect of property taxes is essentially the same in gentrifying and non-gentrifying neighborhoods ...

The big takeaway is that gentrification has a much bigger effect and poses far bigger risks for renters, who tend to have lower incomes, are subject to rising rents, and can be evicted from their apartments.

"Gentrification Has Virtually No Effect on Homeowners," by Richard Florida, The Atlantic Monthly Group, January 24, 2017.

qualities that began attracting new people in the first place. When success comes to a neighborhood, it does not always come to its established residents, and the displacement of that community is gentrification's most troubling effect.

No one is more vulnerable to the effects of gentrification than renters. When prices go up, tenants are pushed out, whether through natural turnover, rent hikes, or evictions. When buildings are sold, buyers often evict the existing tenants to move in themselves, combine several units, or bring in new tenants at a higher rate. When residents own their homes, they are less vulnerable, and may opt to "cash them in" and move elsewhere. Their options may be limited if there is a regional housing shortage, however, and cash does not always compensate for less tangible losses.

The economic effects of gentrification vary widely, but the arrival of new investment, new spending power, and a new tax base usually result in significant increased economic activity. Rehabilitation, housing development, new shops and restaurants, and new, higher-wage jobs are often part of the picture. Previous residents may benefit from some of this development, particularly in the form of service sector and construction jobs, but much of it may be out of reach to all but the well-educated newcomers. Some local economic activity may also be forced out—either by rising rents or shifting sensibilities. Industrial activities that employ local workers may be viewed as a nuisance or environmental hazard by new arrivals. Local shops may lose their leases under pressure from posh boutiques and restaurants.

Physical changes also accompany gentrification. Older buildings are rehabilitated and new construction occurs. Public improvements—to streets, parks, and infrastructure—may accompany government revitalization efforts or occur as new residents organize to demand public services. New arrivals often push hard to improve the district aesthetically, and may codify new standards through design guidelines, historic preservation legislation, and the use of blight and nuisance laws.

The social, economic, and physical impacts of gentrification often result in serious political conflict, exacerbated by differences in race, class, and culture. Earlier residents may feel embattled, ignored, and excluded from their own communities. New arrivals are often mystified by accusations that their efforts to improve local conditions are perceived as hostile or even racist.

Change—in fortunes, in populations, in the physical fabric of communities—is an abiding feature of urban life. But change nearly always involves winners and losers, and low-income people are rarely the winners. The effects of gentrification vary widely with the particular local circumstances. Residents, community development corporations, and city governments across the country are struggling to manage these inevitable changes to create a win-win situation for everyone involved.

> *"I am from Providence and I want to be back here in Providence. We love Providence, we don't want to be pushed out of our homes."*

Urban Renewal Ignores Affordable Housing

Jack Brook

In the following viewpoint, Jack Brook contends that even those who rejuvenate ailing communities with the best intentions inevitably do a disservice to those communities' residents. Using the city of Providence, Rhode Island, its Everyhome program, and the subsequent Gentrification Is Breaking Our Hearts protest movement to illustrate his point, the author discusses the possible ramifications of city revitalization on its residents. He also argues that revitalizations and gentrifications are a method for "colonizing" neighborhoods with new residents. Brook writes for the College Hill Independent.

As you read, consider the following questions:

1. What is the overall plan of the Everyhome program?
2. Why is revitalization seem as a method of colonization?
3. What other questions and issues have been raised by residents concerned about Everyhome?

"Gentrification Is Breaking Our Hearts: The Affordable Housing Crisis in Providence," by Jack Brook, February 18, 2016. Reprinted by permission.

R oline Burgison has been forced to leave from over ten different houses in South Providence despite never missing a day of rent. A combination of poorly constructed housing, problematic landlords, and most of all, a series of landlord foreclosures has kept her on the move, as was the case with the last house she lived in, on 4080 Public Street.

"My landlord came and got his rent and the next day I get a paper in the mail," Burgison told me, referring to the house on Public Street. "It was the bank from Boston, telling me that my house was up for foreclosure."

Burgison, a 53-year-old American woman and mother of four grown men, used to work as a security guard, but now lives on a fixed Social Security income after suffering a severe back injury from a car accident. The average income required to rent a single family apartment in Providence is over $40,000—yet Burgison receives less than $800 a month, which has made it difficult for her to find, in her words, a "reasonable" place in Providence's South Side.

Despite living on the South Side for 30 years, she recently relocated to Cranston, as it was easier to find a home, though she continues to search for an affordable house in Providence. Since then, the frustrated Burgison has become involved with the Direct Action for Rights and Equality (DARE), a Providence-based organization that seeks to empower low-income families in communities of color and give them a voice in social justice issues. Affordable housing is one of DARE's primary concerns.

On the morning of February 11 Burgison shared her story as the first speaker in the DARE demonstration against the mayor's new housing plan, Everyhome. Other protesters crowded behind her outside the mayor's office on the second floor of the Providence City Hall, holding large cardboard cut-outs of broken hearts. The protest's name—Gentrification is Breaking Our Hearts—revealed the fears of many middle class and low-income city residents about Everyhome, a heavily subsidized program designed to clear the city of approximately 650 abandoned and neglected houses.

The program allows investors and local contractors to renovate and redevelop these houses, which the protestors feared would ultimately lead to the displacement of local residents from their neighborhoods. They felt that Everyhome could and should be used as a means to create affordable housing units.

"I am from Providence and I want to be back here in Providence," said Burgison. "We love Providence, we don't want to be pushed out of our homes."

The Illusion of Everyhome

On the surface, the Everyhome plan sounds great: fix up and resell vacant homes which drag down property values and become hotspots for drugs and urban decay. The logistics of the program, however, remain ominously vague and unclear, at least in the minds of Burgison, DARE, and other local activists. They want answers—Who exactly will be receiving these new houses? Will it be the city's low-income residents or wealthy outsiders? And what steps will City Hall take to check what could potentially turn into an unregulated free market, with the redeveloped houses being turned over for maximum profit?

According to Raymond Neirinckx, coordinator for the State of Rhode Island Housing Resources Commission, the real problem with Everyhome is that it lacks a sense of "vision and purpose" for these properties, aside from simply putting them back on the market.

"The community should not suffer indignity of losing homes and then not get the opportunity to recover them," Neirinckx told me. "This should be about a community recovery, not a market recovery."

Although DARE had met with mayor Elorza in early December, the organization feels that its questions about the vision of the program still remain unanswered. The city has not responded to DARE's most ambitious demand—that 50 percent of the houses to be recovered, or around 300, be set aside for very low-income families.

"Everyhome is specifically targeted to vacant and abandoned homes," Evan England, the mayor's press secretary, told me. "It does not require affordable housing, but that city supports that. It is incredibly important, but not necessarily wise to conflate those two priorities."

Malchus Mills, an African-American with a graying beard and a cane, stepped up as the next speaker after Burgison. A 63-year-old disabled war veteran on a fixed income, Mills, too, has been forced out of the city he would like to call home, and lives in Pawtucket instead. What troubles Mills in particular is the lack of community involvement in the mayor's housing plan—one of DARE's main requests is the creation of a community advisory board. According to his press secretary, the mayor rejected this request on the grounds that the court system, which oversees the investors who redevelop the houses, has ultimate authority on that matter and would have to consent. In other words, it's not his problem.

"How can you say you are helping the community when you're not talking to us in any way?" Mills thundered. "In conjunction with Valentine's Day, Mayor Elorza, our love affair with you is over." He ripped a red heart in half and tossed it on the floor, to the resonant applause of the twenty-five protesters, a mix of students and older folks from across all demographics, many of whom wore red DARE t-shirts.

Concluded Joe Buchanan, 63, the vice president of DARE and the protest's final speaker: "We'll be back, five, six days in a row if we have to, Mayor Elorza, because it's our city hall. We put you in here, we can take you out too."

Gentrification as Colonization

While no one on either side believes that abandoned houses should remain in their present state, members of DARE consider healthy urban development a matter of recognizing the voices of the poor in the redevelopment of their neighborhoods and a prime opportunity to construct much needed affordable housing units alongside market-priced ones. One solution Neirinckx suggests is to have the city work with the Providence Housing Authority to see if residents in public housing can become homeowners of redeveloped properties, which would free up space in the crowded public housing for other families. But since Everyhome provides no incentives or policies for any such initiative—indeed, affordable housing is explicitly not one of its priorities—this opportunity will likely be lost.

Ironically, Mayor Elorza wrote his thesis at Roger Williams University School of Law, in 2007, on "Absentee Landlords, Rent Control and Healthy Gentrification: A Policy Proposal to Deconcentrate the Poor in Urban America." In it, Elorza writes that, "the focus of advocates for the poor should be on intervening at a particular point in the vicious cycle [of gentrification] that will convert it into a virtuous cycle that creates 'cumulative upward movement' in the living conditions of the poor." Which, in a sense, is exactly what DARE is seeking to do—intervene in the process of redeveloping neighborhoods full of abandoned houses and ensure the residents of those neighborhoods have a voice and the chance to live in these redevelopments.

Elorza also writes that many policy interventions do not "address the root causes [of gentrification] as they fail to develop the poor's capacity to determine their own fate at the local neighborhood level." Rotondo and Mills emphasize that the advisory board DARE proposes would be a way for the interests of the city to align with those of the communities it is supposedly seeking to help.

"At the end of the day, gentrification is a colonization tactic," says Christopher Rotondo, an organizer for DARE. "It's a way to move people out of a space that you now desire. Neighborhoods change all the time and the way they change and why is based on political power."

This same political power could be harnessed to ensure that much-needed change takes places. It appears that Elorza's ideas are now being put to test—the only question is whether he and the city will act on them.

The Roots of the Crisis

The bitterness and resentment manifest in the DARE protest are rooted in the rising crisis of the affordable housing deficiency in Rhode Island, nowhere more apparent than in Providence. While by law ten percent of Providence's housing must be set aside as long-term affordable (i.e. for families earning 80 percent or less of the city's median income), a 2015 housing report by Roger Williams University concluded that this benchmark was woefully insufficient. In 2014, about fifteen percent of houses in Providence were considered affordable housing, but even so, households earning $30,000 or less—about half of those renting—were not able to rent an average-priced 2-bedroom apartment in any Rhode Island city or town.

Even worse, in the last fifteen years, Rhode Island has had the second smallest increase in housing units among all states, and rental vacancies are at a 20-year low. It's harder than ever for middle and lower class families to find housing, let alone something affordable. And for those who do, the cost of living in a house proves to be a drain on resources—according to the Roger Williams report, 57 percent of Providence renters spend more than 30 percent of their income on housing costs. This is well above the national average of 49 percent reported by the National Low Income Housing Coalition.

Because Providence is already experiencing an affordable-housing crisis, Rotondo believes that Everyhome could exacerbate the situation by serving as a vehicle for gentrification. After an investor is allowed to redevelop a property, the entire dynamic of a neighborhood can change, sending a ripple effect throughout the local community, usually in the form of much higher rents. It is true that in many ways this change can be positive—a cumulative decrease in poverty (ideally by helping increase the well being of the poor, as opposed to simply forcing them out) and an increase in businesses and urban benefits like parks. Moreover, there have been a variety of controversial studies, including one recently released by the California government, which have revealed that development does not necessarily force the majority of residents out of the neighborhood and can correlate with reduced rent prices in the long-term.

But Rotondo says that while redevelopment has many potential benefits, what concerns him most is the lack of agency granted to the poor in these neighborhoods. It's all well and good to seek to eradicate poverty through redevelopment, he adds, but the voices of those who will be affected, for better or worse, should be heard in the process of reshaping the neighborhood.

The Powers That Be

There are four abandoned houses in a stretch of two blocks on Greeley Street in South Providence. Two on Tell Street by Federal Hill, another on Mangolia, and more on Ellery—all addresses on a list which the city has provided DARE of Olneyville and South Providence houses slated for redevelopment. These geographically consolidated properties are exactly the sort that, when redeveloped, have the potential to fundamentally alter the landscape of their neighborhoods.

"A lot of these properties are not going to be profitable," Rotondo told me. "Part of the idea that's been floating around is to bulk sell units to national investors."

The properties would then likely become high-priced single-family homes, as opposed to affordably priced multi-family structures, he adds. There are millions of dollars in various funds in the Everyhome "toolbox," and all are open to investors regardless of whether the goal of their projects is to produce affordable housing or not. Without proper incentives, why would any profit-minded investor create affordable housing? The subsidies could have been set aside solely to encourage affordable housing, a policy the city failed to mandate.

Abandoned houses are currently redeveloped through a receivership program, in which a court-appointed attorney is paid to raise money to hire contractors and fix up properties before selling. The attorney gets to keep the profits of the sale, along

RISING RENTS

This is interesting, but probably not very surprising: according to a report released last week, the black population in the city's "gentrifying" communities—places like Central Harlem, Brownsville, Bedford-Stuyvesant and Morrisania, just to name a few—declined by seven percent from 1990 to 2010.

For the purposes of this column, we're defining "gentrifying" communities as those with predominantly black and brown residents, most of whom have low incomes, that have suddenly become attractive to white folks as prices in more upscale parts of the city trend out of reach.

As these communities became hip, gentrified—whatever you want to call it, local development followed and brought with it higher rents, Starbucks and fewer affordable housing options for black and brown folks of low and modest economic means.

Oddly, the same report, by New York University's Furman Center, seemed to downplay the effects of gentrification in changing the racial and socioeconomic makeup of these neighborhoods. Instead, the report argued that rapidly rising rents across the city, in gentrifying and non-gentrifying communities alike, were a larger problem impacting the city's housing affordability crisis and therefore should be the focus of policy change.

with being paid for his work by the government. The problem, Rotondo says, is that there is no entity outside City Hall that can help oversee the actions of the receivers.

"Who better knows what's going on in a community than the people who are there everyday?" Mills says. "These are the people who should be involved in the decision."

It is clear that there is a deep mistrust between many low-income Providence residents and their city government, in no small part due to a profound lack of transparency. Minorities and low-income residents don't have many reasons to believe that investors and developers have their best interests in mind—for instance, in 2014, Santander Bank was sued by the city of Providence for

Imagine a family, who together make $30,000 a year, living in a $1,000-a-month apartment in a gentrifying neighborhood. Their rent is 40 percent of their income. Now suppose they leave. Since the neighborhood is gentrifying, they may well be replaced by a new family with a much higher income—maybe one that can really afford to pay $2,000 for that same apartment. And somehow the landlord will find a way to charge them that, or more.

Now imagine a household making $30,000 a year and paying $1,000 a month for an apartment in a persistently poor neighborhood. That's still 40 percent of their income. But when they move, they will probably be replaced by a new family that makes about the same income. And that new $30,000-a-year family will pay something like $1,500 a month (because the landlord will raise the rent on vacancy, legally or otherwise) which is 60 percent of their income.

If we are to preserve this city as a place where people with a range of incomes can live and raise their families, then we must close loopholes in the state rent laws that permit deregulation and excessive rent increases to displace families and weaken our rent stabilization system.

"Gentrification, Rising Rents and the City's Changing Housing Landscape," by David R. Jones, Community Service Society, May 19, 2016.

redlining. When residents feel they are not able to participate in public policy initiatives or hold the political leadership accountable to their promises, civic relationships inevitably corrode, creating a dangerous division between those with power and those without.

Creating a Witness for the Community

Joe Buchanan, 63, rested on the steps of City Hall after the protest. His beige collared shirt poked out from underneath a black one which read, in sparkling blue and red letters, "President of the Streets." A South Providence resident his whole life, Buchanan has been an advocate for social justice since he was 12-years-old.

"We will fight any fight we need to fight, we'll take any action we need to take to get done what needs to be done," Buchanan says, reflecting on the day's protest and emphasizing each word with a thump of his cane. "He [the Mayor] thinks that all we [DARE] do is rabblerouse, but what we really do is create a witness for our community. We're not going away, because community doesn't go away."

But it very well could, if Everyhome turns out to create a cycle of harmful gentrification, one in which low-income residents lack agency in the redevelopment of their own neighborhoods.

"Two trends accompany rising rents in the United States—growing urban inequality and a widening gap between the demand and supply of affordable housing."

The Consequences of Displacement by Gentrification Are Harmful

Justin Feldman

In the following viewpoint, Justin Feldman addresses the two consequences of gentrification and rising rents in gentrified neighborhoods: a widening gap between supply and demand for rental units, and a growing inequality between lower- and higher-income residents in cities. The author presents some research that seems to argue against the rates of displacement of lower-income people in gentrifying neighborhoods, as well as research that seems to indicate that these residents are being displaced as neighborhoods become more desirable. Feldman is a social epidemiologist at the NYU School of Medicine Department of Population Health.

As you read, consider the following questions:

1. The author presents several different research studies. Do they result in the same overall conclusions?
2. What are some of the benefits and drawbacks of gentrification when it comes to low-income residents?
3. What is the advantage of this article's presentation of several different studies, instead of the author's own original research?

The cost of renting a home has increased throughout the United States in recent years, most notably in urban areas. According to an April 2014 analysis by Zillow Real Estate Research, between 2000 and 2014 median household income rose 25%, while rents increased by nearly 53%. The analysis also found that residents of Los Angeles, Miami, San Francisco and New York paid the highest portions of their income on rent—in Los Angeles, the figure was 35%. The US Department of Housing and Urban Development considers housing to be unaffordable when its costs exceed 30% of a family's income. A 2014 report from Harvard's Joint Center for Housing Studies found that just over half of US households paid more than 30% of their income toward rent in 2013, up from 38% of households in 2000.

Two trends accompany rising rents in the United States—growing urban inequality and a widening gap between the demand and supply of affordable housing. A 2014 Brookings Institution analysis of Census data found that economic inequality was higher in cities than the country as a whole, and a 2013 study from Cornell and Stanford determined that income-based neighborhood segregation rose between 1970 and 2009 (racial segregation slowly decreased from very high initial levels, however). Furthermore, an Urban Institute analysis found that for every 100 "extremely low-income" households in 2012, only 29 affordable rental units were available—a drop from 37 in 2000. Of the affordable units that are available, most involve federal housing assistance such as Section 8 vouchers, the Low-Income Housing Tax Credit program and government-owned public housing.

Background History

The term "gentrification" often arises in conversations about urban inequality and the increased cost of rental housing. Sociologist Ruth Glass coined the term in 1964, defining it as a process by which a neighborhood's "original working-class occupiers are displaced" by influx of higher-income newcomers. More broadly, gentrification refers to a process of neighborhood change involving the migration of wealthier residents into poorer neighborhoods and increased economic investment. Since the term appeared in the lexicon, scholars have debated both its precise meaning and the phenomenon's effects on society—particularly whether the process harms or benefits the original residents of gentrifying neighborhoods.

In the 2000s, researchers published some of the first longitudinal studies quantifying trends in gentrification. Challenging the long-held beliefs of many urban geographers, these studies generally found that the extent to which gentrification displaced low-income residents was limited. In 2005, Lance Freeman of Columbia University published an influential nationwide study that found that low-income residents of gentrifying urban neighborhoods were only slightly more likely to leave than those in non-gentrifying neighborhoods—1.4% versus 0.9%. Many journalists and some policymakers took the study to mean that gentrification had a negligible social cost while benefiting poor residents through improvements to neighborhoods—for example, an article by *USA Today* was headlined "Studies: Gentrification a Boost for Everyone." However, in 2008 Freeman stated that more research was needed: "The empirical evidence [on gentrification] is surprisingly thin on some questions and inconclusive on others."

Benefits or Drawbacks?

Recent studies of neighborhood change have examined other effects of gentrification on low-income residents. Research published in 2010 and 2011 found evidence that gentrification could boost income for low-income residents who remained and also raised their level of housing-related satisfaction. Examinations of gentrification's effects on crime have found mixed results, with a 2010 study of Los Angeles neighborhoods showing a rise in crime and a 2011 Chicago-based study showing a decrease (with the exception of street robberies in majority-black neighborhoods, which increased). A 2014 study from Grace Hwang and Robert J. Sampson of Harvard found that black neighborhoods were less likely to be gentrified than those with significant Asian or Latino populations.

Even if the proportion of low-income residents displaced by gentrification is low, research indicates that the aggregate number displaced can be high and the consequences of displacement particularly harmful. A 2006 study estimated that about 10,000 households were displaced by gentrification each year in New York City. Follow-up interviews found that among those displaced, many ended up living in overcrowded apartments, shelters or even became homeless. Further, there may be long-term political consequences for low-income residents of gentrified neighborhoods—a 2014 study found poor neighborhoods with rich enclaves spent less on public programs, for example.

Research Deficits

The major studies on gentrification share several important limitations: They have not consistently examined the fate of displaced low-income residents; they do not look at the effects of gentrification over multiple decades; and most use data from the 1980s and 1990s—preceding major increases in rental prices throughout the 2000s and before the Great Recession. There is also no consensus on how to measure gentrification, so existing studies may be missing important demographic transitions in

US neighborhoods. More research is needed about the extent of urban displacement and the social effects of gentrification in the contemporary United States.

The following is a recommended selection of studies on gentrification and its effects:

"Displacement or Succession? Residential Mobility in Gentrifying Neighborhoods"
Freeman, Lance. *Urban Affairs Review*, 2005. Vol. 40, Issue 4. doi: 10.1177/1078087404273341.

Findings: "Overall, the models suggest at most a modest link between gentrification and displacement. The relationship between mobility and gentrification is not statistically significant. Although displacement was significantly related to gentrification, the substantive size of this relationship is very small, as indicated by the predicted probabilities. Finally, poor renters do not appear to be especially susceptible to displacement or elevated rates of mobility. Taken together, the results would not seem to imply that displacement is the primary mechanism through which gentrifying neighborhoods undergo socioeconomic change. Nevertheless, it is true that gentrification was related to displacement in this analysis, contrary to the findings of Vigdor (2002) and Freeman and Braconi (2004)."

"Divergent Pathways of Gentrification: Racial Inequality and the Social Order of Renewal in Chicago Neighborhoods"
Hwang, Jackelyn; Sampson, Robert. *American Sociological Review*, 2014. doi: 10.1177/0003122414535774.

Abstract: "Gentrification has inspired considerable debate, but direct examination of its uneven evolution across time and space is rare. We address this gap by developing a conceptual framework on the social pathways of gentrification and introducing a method of systematic social observation using Google Street View to detect visible cues of neighborhood change. We argue that a durable racial hierarchy governs residential selection and, in turn, gentrifying neighborhoods. Integrating census data, police records, prior street-level observations, community surveys, proximity to amenities, and city budget data on capital investments, we find that the pace of gentrification in Chicago from 2007 to 2009 was negatively associated with the concentration of blacks and Latinos in neighborhoods that either showed signs of gentrification or were adjacent and still disinvested in 1995. Racial composition has a threshold effect, however, attenuating gentrification when the share of blacks in a neighborhood is greater than 40 percent. Consistent with theories of neighborhood stigma, we also find that collective perceptions of disorder, which are higher in poor minority neighborhoods, deter gentrification, while observed disorder does not. These results help explain the reproduction of neighborhood racial inequality amid urban transformation."

"How Low-Income Neighborhoods Change: Entry, Exit and Enhancement"

Gould Ellen, Ingrid; O'Regan, Katherine M. *Regional Science and Urban Economics*, March 2011. Vol. 41, Issue 2. doi: 10.1016/j. regsciurbeco.2010.12.005.

Findings: "The picture our analyses paint of neighborhood change is one in which original residents are much less harmed than is typically assumed. They do not appear to be displaced in the course of change, they experience modest gains in income during the process, and they are more satisfied with their neighborhoods in the wake of the change. To be sure, some individual residents are undoubtedly hurt by neighborhood change; but in aggregate, the consequences of neighborhood change—at least as it occurred in the 1990s—do not appear to be as dire as many assume."

"The Right to Stay Put, Revisited: Gentrification and Resistance to Displacement in New York City"

Newman, Kathe; Wyly, Elvin K. *Urban Studies*, January 2006. Vol. 43, Issue 1. doi: 10.1080/00420980500388710.

Findings: "We found that between 8,300 and 11,600 households per year were displaced in New York City between 1989 and

2002, slightly lower than the total number identified in earlier estimates. However, our displacement rates are slightly higher, reaching between 6.6% and 9.9% of all local moves among renter households. We expect that both figures underestimate actual displacement, perhaps substantially, because the [New York City Housing and Vacancy Survey] does not include displaced households that left New York City, doubled up with other households, became homeless, or entered the shelter system— all of which were identified as widespread practices in the field interviews. The dataset also misses households displaced by earlier rounds of gentrification and those that will not gain access to the now-gentrified neighbourhoods in the future."

"Who Gentrifies Low-Income Neighborhoods?"

McKinnish, Terra; Walsh, Randall; White, Kirk T. *Journal of Urban Economics*, 2010. Vol. 27, Issue 2. doi: 10.1016/j.jue.2009.08.003.

Findings: "[R]ather than dislocating non-white households, gentrification of predominantly black neighborhoods creates neighborhoods that are attractive to middle-class black households, particularly those with children or with elderly householders. One reasonable interpretation [...] is that because these neighborhoods are experiencing income gains, but also more racially diverse than established middle-class neighborhoods, they are desirable locations for black middle-class households. In contrast, for the gentrifying tracts with low black populations, we find evidence of disproportionate exit of black high school graduates. It is possible that in these neighborhoods, for black high school graduates, the rising housing costs are not offset by the same benefits of gentrification as in the predominantly black neighborhoods. Despite the exit of black high school graduates, in-migration of this group is sufficient to increase its proportion of the population slightly in these tracts, suggesting some sorting among households in this group with different neighborhood preferences. Perhaps even in the predominantly black neighborhoods, displacement has not occurred yet, but will in the future. It is of course, impossible for us to address this empirically. However, we point out that the neighborhoods we define as gentrified have already experienced massive income growth (in absolute and percentage terms), yet still have very sizeable fractions of non-white and non-college educated households, and sizeable in-migration of these same demographic groups. These facts alone suggest that the stark gentrification-displacement story was not the norm during the 1990's."

"Moving In/Out of Brussels' Historical Core in the Early 2000s: Migration and the Effects of Gentrification"
Van Criekingen, Mathieu. *Urban Studies*, 2009. Vol. 46, Issue 4. doi: 10.1177/0042098009102131.

Abstract: "Exploring migration dynamics associated with gentrification is particularly important in order to shed light on the nature and contested effects of such processes. Quite paradoxically, however, this aspect remains under-investigated in the gentrification literature. This paper explores the migratory dimensions of gentrification in Brussels' historical core, hence offering a view from a city wherein current rounds of middle-class reinvestment of inner urban space operate under circumstances that partially contrast with those reported from more prominent global cities. Findings stress that educated young adults living alone and renting from private landlords are predominant among both in- and out-movers to or from Brussels' historical core, suggesting in turn that renting in a gentrifying area is for most of them associated with a transitional step in their housing career. In addition, findings indicate that displacement of vulnerable residents is a limited but actual constituent of the migration dynamics in Brussels' historical core and point to other harmful consequences of gentrification in the area. In Brussels, gentrification and its effects operate under circumstances associated with the preponderance of a poorly regulated private rental housing market in the city's inner neighbourhoods."

"More Coffee, Less Crime? The Relationship Between Gentrification and Neighborhood Crime Rates in Chicago, 1991 to 2005"

Papachristos, Andrew; Smith, Chris M.; Scherer, Mary L.; Fugiero, Melissa A. *City & Community*, September 2011. Vol. 10, Issue 3. doi: 10.1111/j.1540-6040.2011.01371.x.

Abstract: "This study examines the relationship between gentrification and neighborhood crime rates by measuring the growth and geographic spread of one of gentrification's most prominent symbols: coffee shops. The annual counts of neighborhood coffee shops provide an on-the-ground measure of a particular form of economic development and changing consumption patterns that tap into central theoretical frames within the gentrification literature. Our analysis augments commonly used Census variables with the annual number of coffee shops in a neighborhood to assess the influence of gentrification on three-year homicide and street robbery counts in Chicago. Longitudinal Poisson regression models with neighborhood fixed effects reveal that gentrification is a racialized process, in which the effect of gentrification on crime is different for White gentrifying neighborhoods than for Black gentrifying neighborhoods. An increasing number of coffee shops in a neighborhood is associated with declining homicide rates for White, Hispanic, and Black neighborhoods; however, an increasing number of coffee shops is associated with increasing street robberies in Black gentrifying neighborhoods."

"Endogenous Gentrification and Housing Price Dynamics"

Guerreri, Veronica; Hartley, Daniel; Hurst, Erik. NBER Working Paper No. 16237, July 2010. doi: 10.3386/w16237.

Abstract: "In this paper, we begin by documenting substantial variation in house price growth across neighborhoods within a city during city wide housing price booms. We then present a model which links house price movements across neighborhoods within a city and the gentrification of those neighborhoods in response to a city wide housing demand shock. A key ingredient in our model is a positive neighborhood externality: individuals like to live next to richer neighbors. This generates an equilibrium where households segregate based upon their income. In response to a city wide demand shock, higher income residents will choose to expand their housing by migrating into the poorer neighborhoods that directly abut the initial richer neighborhoods. The in-migration of the richer residents into these border neighborhoods will bid up prices in those neighborhoods causing the original poorer residents to migrate out. We refer to this process as 'endogenous gentrification.' Using a variety of data sets and using Bartik variation across cities to identify city level housing demand shocks, we find strong empirical support for the model's predictions."

Periodical and Internet Sources Bibliography

The following articles have been selected to supplement the diverse views presented in this chapter.

Detroit Journalism Cooperative, "What Gentrification? Much of Detroit Is Getting Worse." Retrieved April 30, 2018. https://www .detroitjournalism.org/2018/01/02/gentrification-much-detroit -getting-worse/.

Sarah Jeong, "Activists Say Airbnb Makes New Orleans Housing Shortage Worse," Verge, March 28, 2018. https://www.theverge .com/2018/3/28/17172946/airbnb-new-orleans-housing-crisis -gentrification-str.

Diane K. Levy, Jennifer Comey, and Sandra Padilla, "Keeping the Neighborhood Affordable: A Handbook of Housing Strategies for Gentrifying Areas," Urban Institute, 2006. https://www.urban .org/sites/default/files/publication/50796/411295-Keeping-the -Neighborhood-Affordable.PDF.

Brentin Mock, "In Search of Answers on Gentrification," *CityLab*, November 3, 2016. https://www.citylab.com/equity/2016/11/in -search-of-answers-on-gentrification/506267/.

Michelle Robertson, "A Citywide Crisis in Gentrification? New SF Residents Make Far More Money than Those Leaving," SF Gate, April 16, 2018. https://www.sfgate.com/expensive-san-francisco /article/Who-s-moving-to-San-Francisco-The-rich-the-12805760 .php.

Adam Rogers, "A Bid to Solve California's Housing Crisis Could Redraw How Cities Grow," *Wired*, February 7, 2018. https://www .wired.com/story/scott-weiner-california-housing-bill-cities/.

Melanie Sevcenko, "Un-gentrifying Portland: Scheme Helps Displaced Residents Come Home," *Guardian* (Manchester), March 1, 2018. https://www.theguardian.com/cities/2018/mar/01/portland-anti -gentrification-housing-scheme-right-return.

Patrick Sisson, "If California's the Future, Why Are So Many Leaving?," Curbed, February 27, 2018. https://www.curbed.com /2018/2/27/17058006/california-housing-crisis-rent-migration -texas.

OPPOSING
VIEWPOINTS®
SERIES

CHAPTER 3

Does Gentrification Diminish a Community's History and Culture?

Chapter Preface

M any city neighborhoods are centers for ethnic culture, a place where people share a common history and can draw on the social capital of their culture as support. They share celebrations and events, foods, lifestyles, and values. But what happens to the history and culture of a neighborhood community when gentrification occurs?

It is often argued that gentrification can diversify a neighborhood, adding residents of different income levels, ages, and backgrounds. Often ethnic neighborhoods are marketed to young urban professionals as being hip and more authentic than all-white, middle- and upper-class neighborhoods. Diversity is used as a selling point, and yet once a neighborhood begins to undergo gentrification, the very people who made it diverse may be forced out and scattered in other sections of the city.

It might seem like an opportunity for new groups to mix with existing groups and create even more diversity. Ideally, all these groups would interact on a daily basis, share their cultures and viewpoints, and work together for a better neighborhood. But some studies find that there is still a segregation in place, especially in neighborhood institutions like churches, recreation centers, restaurants and bars, and clubs. There can be losses in political power as well when the new residents displace the old and the representation changes. And sometimes new residents, while saying they want cultural diversity, find that they are not comfortable in ethnic groups and may stay separate from the neighborhood's dominant cultures.

Neighborhoods may also lose their history when they become gentrified. Historic preservation may occur as buildings are renovated, but sometimes it comes at the cost of institutions and stores that were previously centers for the neighborhood residents. Gentrification may save structures and historic places, but it can destroy what made those places historic or notable in the first place.

> "Because social capital creates value
> for the people who are connected, the
> urban regeneration team should be
> concerned about how out-migration
> and relocation will impact economic
> opportunities for the population."

Gentrification Can Sever Social Ties

World Bank

In the following viewpoint, the World Bank argues that one of the common consequences of gentrification, beyond displacing residents who can't afford to remain, is a loss of social capital. Social capital is a complex network of relationships and interactions that weave residents together and enable them to function in daily life. The author discusses the need for resettlement of residents and how to minimize the impact of that displacement on the neighborhood fabric. The World Bank is an international financial institution that provides loans to countries for capital projects in an effort to end poverty.

"Managing the Potential Undesirable Impacts of Urban Regeneration: Gentrification and Loss of Social Capital," The World Bank Group, January 1, 2016. https://openknowledge. worldbank.org/handle/10986/24377. Licensed under CC BY 3.0 IGO.

As you read, consider the following questions:

1. What is social capital, and why is it important?
2. Why is resettlement of residents sometimes necessary in revitalizing a neighborhood?
3. What are some things that can be done to minimize the impact of displacement?

One of the unintended consequences of urban regeneration is gentrification. Gentrification is a shift in an urban community toward wealthier residents and businesses, with consequent increases in property values. Gentrification is typically the result of investment in a community by real estate development businesses, local government, or community activists. It can and often does spur economic development, attract businesses, and lower crime rates. In addition to these potential benefits, gentrification can lead to some adverse population migration trends in which poorer residents are displaced by wealthier newcomers. In a community undergoing gentrification, the average income increases and the average family size decreases. Poorer pregentrification residents who are unable to pay the increased rents or property taxes may be driven out. Consequently, new businesses arrive to the area, which can afford the increased commercial rent. They cater specifically to a more affluent base of consumers—further increasing the appeal to higher-income migrants and decreasing accessibility to the poor.

When designing an urban regeneration project, the social aspects of the initiative should be as important as environmental and economic considerations and should be fully taken into account at the outset of project preparation. Community engagement is one way to discover, define, and address social issues pertaining to the regeneration project. As such, people with the right skill set are needed for the job.

Gentrification is a very complex matter and there are numerous arguments for and against it, as well as its social consequences for the community. It should be noted that whereas some scholars have negative views about gentrification, others simply accept it as a market reality. Some others have criticized it as social restructuring by the state or even "displacement" (Snel and others 2011). Gentrification could be led by the market or the state. Indeed, urban regeneration policies implemented by central or local governments can have a tremendous impact on gentrification, as well as on the lives of the original residents. In this section, we focus on a variety of tools that cities have used to address the problem of gentrification and access to affordable housing.

A second unwanted consequence of regeneration projects— related to gentrification and out-migration of the original population—is the loss of social capital, or community ties. Broadly speaking, social capital can be defined as a set of social norms of conduct, knowledge, mutual obligations and expectations, and reciprocity and trust that are widespread within a given region or community. The concept is also connected with social networks (Colantonio and Dixon 2011).

Social capital refers to the collective value of all "social networks" (who people know) and the inclinations that arise from these networks to do things for each other (norms of reciprocity). The term "social capital" emphasizes a wide variety of specific benefits that flow from the trust, reciprocity, information, and cooperation associated with social networks. Because social capital creates value for the people who are connected, the urban regeneration team should be concerned about how out-migration and relocation will impact economic opportunities for the population. For example, the loss of access to information flows can disrupt the relocated population by reducing opportunities to learn about jobs.

The case of Anacostia in Washington, DC, offers a good example of how to manage gentrification in the targeted neighborhood. For example, the Arthur Capper/Carrollsburg development guaranteed one-for-one replacement of demolished public housing units in the same footprint as the original development. At the Southwest Waterfront, the planning effort was crystalized in an agreement between the developer and the long-term residents by which the tenants received affordable units in the new housing development. The Yards project also includes affordable housing units.

Tools to Mitigate the Undesirable Social Impacts of Urban Regeneration

How can project managers avoid these undesirable social outcomes? This section outlines some tools that have been used in different contexts to minimize the negative impacts of urban regeneration projects.

Successful urban resettlement requires attention to density and diversity, usually in a context of rapid change. High population density is an obvious hallmark of urban life. Although population density in the urban landscape creates opportunities (such as concentrated demand for goods and services, employment, and land and other natural resources), it also creates problems, such as pollution and waste disposal. Resettlement in urban areas is often expensive because public infrastructure must be built, rehabilitated, or upgraded in an area where people are already living and working. As a consequence, even projects acquiring little land in urban areas can generate a fairly large displacement. Furthermore, even a temporary loss of land or other assets can cause severe and costly impacts.

When Is Resettlement Justified?

Even though population displacement should be avoided when possible, some urban regeneration projects might require resettlement in order to be implemented. The need for resettlement should be looked at from a cost-benefit point of view. Project planners should attempt to understand the project's potential winners and losers. Potential gains can be manifested in terms of property value increases, tax revenues, and private investment in the area that might not otherwise occur. Potential losses may involve displaced populations and businesses, as well as hardship in accessing jobs due to distance. Some positive aspects of the regeneration projects may be hard to quantify. This includes improvements in the quality of life, quality of urban environment, and an improved image for the city. But the negative impacts, such as resettlement, will be observed by the community. The point is that resettlement is only justified if the regeneration project brings large enough gains for the city to outweigh the losses of the impacted population. In many cases, project teams can develop win-win situations, whereby the resettled population lives in improved conditions. See, for example, box on vertical resettlement in India.

Early resettlement planning is always advised. This is especially important as resettlement costs can escalate quickly in urban areas. A good practice is to base the initial project design on an assessment of social and demographic conditions and then revise it to incorporate information from public consultations. Timing is crucial, because resettlement mistakes can be especially costly in urban projects. Careful, early, and participatory planning is necessary to later avoid major revisions in respect to investments during implementation. It also helps to ensure that the displaced populations accept resettlement conditions.

Resettlement itself is invariably complex. The many tasks to be performed range from urban planning to the issuance of land acquisition notices, to provision of resettlement-site infrastructure, to payment of compensation, to provision of employment or other forms of economic rehabilitation. A substantial number of governmental agencies scattered horizontally across several jurisdictional levels are therefore likely to be involved in any operation.

Resettlement can be an opportunity for low-income communities, as it can help them gain titles to properties they occupy. Resettlement of low-income informal communities often provides opportunities for moving beyond the narrow mitigation of adverse impacts to promoting community development, security of tenure, and rational land use.

The Principle of Minimizing Displacement

Technical considerations are fundamentally important in project design, but they are not the only factors to consider. Environmental and social factors are also important. In dense urban settings, minimizing displacement is likely to reduce overall project costs and make project implementation easier. From the social perspective, resettlement costs may not simply be directly proportional to the number of displaced people. Costs depend on the type and degree of impacts. Compensating a large number of people for minor or partial land acquisition may cost far less than physically relocating a few people and providing them with income-restoring alternatives.

In urban projects, minimizing both the number of displaced people and the severity of resettlement impacts—especially residential relocation and changes in employment—is necessary. Another good practice is to minimize the distance of any necessary relocation: families moving less than a kilometer in the city often find that their lives, community ties, and livelihoods are much less disrupted than those moving greater distances. The following are some of the steps normally taken in the early stages of project design:

- Send out information about project objectives and potential impacts within the project area. Given the diversity of tenure arrangements, a good practice is to supplement legally required notification with other public announcements to ensure that renters, owners, and others are informed about the project.
- Conduct a census of project impacts and publicly display the results.
- Solicit information from potential displaced persons regarding valuation of losses and preferences for possible resettlement options.
- Send out information regarding compensation rates and other entitlements. Also include the resettlement implementation schedule.

- Form a community-based committee to coordinate with the project resettlement agency.
- Require careful coordination of several layers of government and multiple line agencies for successful design and implementation of urban projects.

Compensation Methods

The rules for compensation will be formulated by each country and should follow existing rules, laws, and procedures. The general notion is that compensation should be fair, which means that it should cover both the expropriated assets and rehabilitation measures to help restore incomes or standards of living (including foregone income). It is key to have in place a set of procedures for asset valuation. The World Bank policy for resettlement establishes that compensation should be paid at replacement cost. The alternative of replacing at market cost may not be fair in countries in which land markets do not function well and prices are distorted.

The census of affected people should identify residential and commercial tenure arrangements for people with and without formal rights, such as residents claiming ownership of private land but lacking legal title. Other individuals and groups to consider include tenants, squatters on public lands, squatters in public safety zones, owners of enterprises lacking licenses or property titles, marketers, and mobile and itinerant vendors. Consideration also needs to be given to issues involving drains, riverbeds, and rights-of-way. Furthermore, urban residential and commercial areas in most developing countries often have informal (unauthorized or unlicensed) economic activity. The displacement of informal enterprises can be disastrous for people who derive their incomes from them. The loss of such information enterprises may also deprive communities of access to products or services. Potentially displaced formal and informal enterprises should be identified and appropriate remedies devised.

In many urban projects, the identification of replacement land and provision of replacement housing are serious constraints. Regarding land, the calculation of replacement cost is made more complex by gross disparities in land prices or, in some cities, the absence of a functional land market. The provision of replacement housing is often a crucial ingredient in urban resettlement planning. Remedies usually take some variant of two basic forms. In some cases, those losing their housing are relocated to newly-developed housing sites. In other cases, projects follow "fill-in" resettlement strategies, in which displaced people obtain existing vacant housing. Alternatively, new housing is constructed on vacant lots scattered throughout several areas. Land replacement, whether in kind or in cash, recognizes not only the quantity of land acquired but also its characteristics, such as location and productive capacity. For land in urban areas, location accounts for great differences in value. Because of its centrality, a parcel of land in the inner city may be worth many times the same sized plot in a peripheral area. Such an inner-city plot may also have advantages of location that cannot be compensated by a larger plot in a more distant area.

The Ahmedabad case study provides good lessons about how not to deal with resettlement. The Ahmedabad Municipal Corporation, the agency in charge of project implementation, proposed that the relocation of the project-affected households be done on municipal-owned land sites far from the riverfront, where the affected households were located. This was justified on the basis of project costs because the land used for relocation would come from the municipality through its land bank and not the project itself. This saved the Sabarmati Riverfront Development Corporation a considerable amount of resources. However, many of the informal settlements were relocated to residential complexes far from the city center. The project was also accused of not providing resettlement compensation to all affected parties.

| "*Preservation also tends to focus on 'aspects of history that are relatively narrow.*'"

Efforts Can Be Made to Retain a Neighborhood's Identity

Rachel Kaufman

In the following viewpoint, Rachel Kaufman presents some possible ways to maintain and foster cultural heritage and historic preservation in neighborhoods undergoing revitalization or gentrification. While some residents may be skeptical or think that government programs designed to maintain historic properties or centers are taking too much control of their neighborhood, in San Francisco, some of these cultural heritage measures are working. Kaufman is a journalist covering transportation, sustainability, science, and technology. Her writing has appeared in Inc., National Geographic News, Scientific American, *and more.*

As you read, consider the following questions:

1. What are some of the new ideas being used to preserve culture in revitalized neighborhoods?
2. What do critics say about traditional historic preservation?
3. What is so special about Japantown in San Francisco?

"Giving Communities the Historic Preservation They Want," by Rachel Kaufman, Next City, April 22, 2016. Reprinted by permission.

San Francisco's Board of Supervisors adopted a resolution last week to designate a Cultural Heritage District in the South of Market neighborhood honoring the neighborhood's Filipino residents and heritage.

SoMa Pilipinas is more than symbolic: It's a tool that will possibly affect land use and economic development within the boundaries of the district, according to Supervisor Jane Kim, who authored the ordinance.

"It is not just about preserving our history and our culture. It is also talking about how we can use land use controls and economic development tools to make sure our community continues to stay in the South of Market for decades to come," Kim told KQED. "We want to ensure our community leaders, our diversity, get to stay in San Francisco."

SoMa Pilipinas is just one of many new ideas San Francisco is experimenting with in an effort to preserve places important to its quickly dwindling minority populations.

Among these experiments are density bonuses to developers who preserve cultural landmarks, and a first-of-its-kind program that helps longtime businesses pay their landlords as rents rise.

"Traditional" historic preservation has its critics, some with understandable concerns. Designating a building or neighborhood historic can lead to gentrification as "preserved" neighborhoods go up in value and become unaffordable to longtime residents.

Preservation also tends to focus on "aspects of history that are relatively narrow," says Donna Graves, an independent historian whose study of San Francisco's forays into this new world of intangible preservation was published in March.

Jim Buckley, a lecturer at MIT who coauthored the study says the city's Legacy Business Historic Preservation Fund, which is currently being implemented, "seems to be popular." It provides grants to long-standing businesses so owners of, say, a community's favorite bookstore can stay afloat, and landlords can get closer to market-rate rents. "These programs are trying to help people who are living and working and using the buildings now," Buckley says.

GENTRIFICATION MAY BE A GOOD THING

Bobby Foster Jr. can often be found reading the paper on a wooden bench outside Murry's grocery store on the corner of Sixth and H streets northeast in Washington, D.C.

Murry's has been an anchor in this neighborhood for decades — during the crack wars of the 1980s and the urban blight that followed, when most other businesses packed up and left. Foster has been somewhat of an anchor, too. He's lived here for 54 years.

But now, this neighborhood and hundreds like it across the country are changing. Every other shop is a new restaurant, high-end salon or bar.

The neighborhood is gentrifying.

That's been a dirty word for 30 years, since the middle and upper classes began returning to many urban cores across the US. It brings up images of neighbors forced out of their homes.

But a series of new studies are now showing that gentrifying neighborhoods may be a boon to longtime residents as well — and that those residents may not be moving out after all.

Gentrification burst into the social consciousness on Aug. 6, 1988, with the Tompkins Square Park riot in New York City's East Village.

The protesters' fury centered on the idea that the poor would be made homeless so the rich could live in their neighborhoods, destroying whatever character they may have had.

Another proposed preservation option is to offer developers a density bonus in exchange for them preserving space inhabited by a business that's long been an anchor in a neighborhood, or community meeting space. Because there's preserving, and then there's preserving in place.

"[That plan] is an attempt to protect places that matter," Graves says. "The … goals would not be reached if … they kept Green Apple Books but moved it to SoMa in the basement of some big luxury condo development. Green Apple Books is part of its neighborhood ecosystem and has contributed to that neighborhood's identity." The details of how the density bonus would work in San Francisco have yet to be worked out, since the measure is only a proposal.

Lance Freeman, the director of the Urban Planning program at Columbia University, says that's what he believed was happening, too. He launched a study, first in Harlem and then nationally, calculating how many people were pushed out of their homes when wealthy people moved in.

"My intuition would be that people were being displaced," Freeman explains, "so they're going to be moving more quickly. I was really aiming to quantify how much displacement was occurring."

Except that's not what he found.

"To my surprise," Freeman says, "it seemed to suggest that people in neighborhoods classified as gentrifying were moving less frequently."

Freeman's work found that low-income residents were no more likely to move out of their homes when a neighborhood gentrifies than when it doesn't.

He says higher costs can push out renters, especially those who are elderly, disabled or without rent-stabilized apartments. But he also found that a lot of renters actually stay—especially if new parks, safer streets and better schools are paired with a job opportunity right down the block.

"Gentrification May Actually Be Boon to Longtime Residents," by Laura Sullivan, National Public Radio Inc., January 22, 2014.

Finally, much of what the city is doing is simply taking community engagement to a more advanced level.

Perhaps the best example of this engagement is in San Francisco's Japantown, where a decade ago the city created a new neighborhood plan in response to a development proposal.

"San Francisco was really excited," says Graves, who was part of the consulting team that worked on the plan. "This was a neighborhood where its history was going to be front and center. To the planners, [the idea was], 'What can we landmark?' And what we … found was the community really didn't want those … preservation tools the planning department was able to offer."

Many communities have reasons to be suspicious of the planning process, Graves adds, but to Japanese-Americans, some who remembered the internments during World War II, the plan reeked of government control. "There was a lot of skepticism to doing anything that put government-sponsored restrictions on property," Graves recalls. "But at that point, [the planning department] didn't feel they had the capacity to address what the community was bringing up, which was, 'What we really want is for you guys to help us preserve our longtime businesses and community events that are really important to us.'"

A revised plan was published in 2013: The Japantown Cultural Heritage and Economic Sustainability Strategy (JCHESS) expanded a list of physical structures deemed culturally important to include intangible items like the annual cherry blossom parade, a children's choir, and the Japanese American Citizens' League's annual crab and spaghetti fundraiser dinner.

Will the San Francisco proposals succeed in halting gentrification and displacement, or prevent neighborhoods from becoming unrecognizable to longtime residents? It's too soon to tell, Graves and Buckley say. Even in SoMa Pilipinas, the new heritage district, the legislation doesn't define what can or can't be done in the district. The city still needs to buckle down and work with community groups to actually create the policies that will inform development in the district.

"Planners would tell you that they've been engaging the community in different ways for decades," says Graves, who acknowledges that the process is difficult. "My perspective is that planning has tried to engage communities on more quantifiable aspects of their experience of urban space. Whether it's the transit questions that might come up, or 'Do we want sidewalks?' But getting at, 'What really gives my neighborhood its identity, and what is crucial to me and my neighbors in maintaining a sense of that neighborhood?' is not a conversation that planners have had."

> *"Most Chinatowns are no longer truly vibrant immigrant communities where people work, live, shop, and socialize. By and large, the people have scattered and working-class Chinese tend not to concentrate in areas like these because there's very few jobs."*

America's Chinatowns Are Losing Their Cultural Identity

Melissa Hung

In the following viewpoint, Melissa Hung argues that across the United States, Chinatowns that were once almost ghettos for ethnic Chinese and other Asian immigrants are falling victim to gentrification. Some Chinatowns have already lost their position as an ethnic center, because long-term residents are unable to afford escalating rents due to gentrification. Some cities are fighting back with organizations dedicated to keeping immigrant culture and history alive, but there is a constant tension between the old Chinatowns and their new revitalized versions. Hung is a journalist covering arts and culture, communities of color, immigration, and criminal justice.

"Chinatowns Across the Country Face Off with Gentrification," by Melissa Hung, National Public Radio Inc., March 15, 2017. Reprinted by permission of Melissa Hung. Originally appeared at NPR.org.

As you read, consider the following questions:

1. What makes Chinatowns vulnerable to gentrification?
2. What are some of the strategies used by the Chinatown CDC?
3. What was the purpose of the "Eat Chinatown" exhibit? What was it meant to highlight?

O n a Friday evening in January, people spilled out of a storefront into an alleyway in San Francisco's Chinatown. Neighborhood business owners, parents with young children, and artists in warm coats chatted with one another. Nearby, youth from a martial arts school practiced with wooden staffs under the alleyway lights.

The occasion was the opening of "Eat Chinatown," a photography exhibit at 41 Ross, a gallery run by the Chinese Culture Center and the Chinatown Community Development Center (Chinatown CDC) in what's considered the oldest alley in the city. For the exhibit, photographer Andria Lo and writer Valerie Luu researched and documented local eateries. The artists focused on legacy businesses that have been in the neighborhood for more than 30 years—such as Capital Restaurant, Hon's Wun-Tun House, and Eastern Bakery—not new upscale additions, such as Mister Jiu's, where a five-course tasting menu costs $105.

Today, Chinatowns like this one are often located in the heart of large cities, making them vulnerable to gentrification.

Originally formed at the edges of downtowns, Chinatowns held on as such commercial and residential areas expanded. Collectively, they represent more than 150 years of immigrant survival since the first wave of Chinese immigration began in the 1850s. "Chinatowns used to be ghettos because of segregation," said Peter Kwong, a professor of urban policy and planning at Hunter College in New York City. "After the 1965 Immigration Act, you have a resurfacing of Chinatowns all throughout the United States, and particularly in the East Coast."

That is far from the case today. An Asian American Legal Defense and Education Fund (AALDEF) study of Chinatowns in three East Coast cities found that the number of white residents in Chinatowns was growing at a faster rate than the overall white population in those cities. "In fact, the white population in Boston and Philadelphia's Chinatown doubled between 2000 and 2010 while the white populations decreased in those cities overall," the authors wrote. In New York's Chinatown, among all racial groups, only the white population had grown in the decade leading to 2013 when the study was released.

Although the details may be different in each Chinatown, the results of rising numbers of white residents is the same: the displacement of low-income immigrants. In Boston, luxury towers have replaced traditional row houses, making the area look more generic and less like Chinatown. In New York, garment factories that used to employ immigrants have been turned into doctors' offices and gyms. Contemporary art galleries have moved in, paying four to five times the rent that was paid by the bakeries and herbal medicine shops they supplanted. In San Francisco, families that cram into single room occupancy (SRO) hotels are being pushed out. Once regarded as the housing of last resort, the rooms are now being marketed to tech workers and students.

Community groups have adopted a variety of strategies to slow gentrification down. Chinatown CDC uses both "hard" and "soft" approaches, said Erika Gee, a senior planner with the organization. The "hard" approach involves organizing residents, bringing media attention to evictions, and advocating for government policies that protect tenants. The "soft" arts and culture approach also touches on community issues, "But it's a celebration of what Chinatown is, what people's experiences are, and doing it in a way that reaches people in a positive way," Gee said.

Chinatown CDC views the "Eat Chinatown" exhibit as a way to tell the stories of the people behind the restaurants and bakeries. For example, the artists wondered why so many of Chinatown's old eateries have a diner aesthetic with counter seating. They learned that due to the Chinese Exclusion Act, men couldn't bring their families from China. Bar seating allowed them to eat full meals by themselves, instead of in the more typical family style.

The ongoing construction of the Central Subway, which will add a terminal in Chinatown, has resulted in a loss of revenue for businesses in its path, and rising concerns for the character of the area. "What is it going to look like after the subway opens? … Are new people going to come in and want different types of things in Chinatown and are willing to pay higher rents? That's an issue that we're watching and concerned about," Gee said.

In Boston, Angie Liou, executive director of Asian Community Development Corporation (ACDC), says Chinatown is being hemmed in from all directions by market-rate developments. "This is a capitalist country. So when the real estate market is hot, it goes quickly in the matter of a few years," she said. The developments drive up property values. "Some people might think, 'That's a bad thing?' What you have to know about Chinatown is that the vast majority of long-term residents are renters," she said. "Home ownership is very, very low here, so when you're talking about renters and property values going up, that's to their detriment." While ACDC can build affordable housing units, those projects take a long time.

A 2016 report found that the median rent in Asian American Pacific Islander (AAPI) neighborhoods increased by 74 percent from 2000 to 2014, compared to the national median rent increase of 53 percent. The report was jointly produced by the National Coalition for Asian Pacific American Community Development and the Council for Native Hawaiian Advancement.

Giles Li is executive director of Boston Chinatown Neighborhood Center (BCNC), which is charged with opening an arts center in a new mixed-use development. This community space will offer programming for residents, old and the new. "There's nothing I can do to slow macroeconomic forces, but maybe if we can get the new residents of Chinatown engaged in this community as residents and as members of this community, maybe that will mitigate the negative impact of gentrification," he said.

Peter Kwong, the Hunter College professor, believes it may be too late for many Chinatowns.

Most Chinatowns are no longer truly vibrant immigrant communities where people work, live, shop, and socialize, he said. "By and large, the people have scattered and working-class Chinese tend not to concentrate in areas like these because there's very few jobs." New York City's Chinatown is the one exception because of a large base of jobs, he said. "We are basically the very last stand," he said of anti-gentrification efforts in New York's Chinatown.

Kwong criticized mixed-income developments as contributing to gentrification. "Even though they may add units, they're still introducing affluent people into a low-income neighborhood," he said. He also questioned the value of arts and culture efforts. "After you see a show, what do you do? What do you do about these people driven out? … You're an artist? These are the things you do? Okay. But don't tell me you are doing something significant in terms of social impact," he said.

Liou thinks interactive arts and culture events such as ACDC's popular outdoor film screenings give residents the opportunity to talk to each other. "I don't think they necessarily understand that there may have been other residents who have been displaced from where they were living, which is not a comfortable conversation, I realize," she said. "I think that's the first step toward some sort of understanding and empathy."

But Kwong argues that the best way to halt displacement is through rezoning and laws that protect tenants. For the past eight years, the Chinatown Working Group, a coalition of more than 50 organizations and residents, has worked on a rezoning plan that would restrict height limits, create anti-harassment laws targeted at landlords, generate affordable housing, and protect small businesses in Chinatown and the Lower East Side. The Department of City

Planning has rejected the plan, but advocates are not giving up. They continue to hold demonstrations on a regular basis outside City Hall to call attention to the issue.

One night in September, the Chinatown Art Brigade, a collective of artists and activists, projected a series of large-scale, multilingual messages onto buildings. The messages were written by residents. "Who did you replace when you opened your gallery? Your bar? When you built your condo??," one of the projections read.

| "Unlike counterparts in other major American cities, the fears of an 'ethnic theme park' have not yet been realized in lower Manhattan."

Chinatowns Are Not Unexplored Frontiers Waiting to Be Conquered

Kartik Naram

In the following excerpted viewpoint, Kartik Naram explores the origins of ethnic Chinatowns and their basis in the immigration attitudes of their time. However, today these neighborhoods have become very valuable real estate as developers rush to transform inner-city neighborhoods. Chinatowns are often marketed to potential residents as being chic, ethnic, and exotic. And yet, characterizing these neighborhoods as exotic often causes white residents to maintain their separateness, even as they live in expensive housing within the area. Chinatowns also become places where others can profit from what is essentially the neighborhood's own social capital. Naram is a law clerk in the complex litigation and trials department at the New York offices of Skadden, Arps, Slate, Meagher & Flom.

"No Place like Home: Racial Capitalism, Gentrification, and the Identity of Chinatown," by Kartik Naram, *Asian American Policy Review*, June 29, 2017. Reprinted by permission.

As you read, consider the following questions:

1. In the original Chinatowns, what were some of the benefits residents gained through their segregation?
2. How do developers "sell" Chinatown neighborhoods to potential residents?
3. How has the neighborhood been "defined by the actions and interests of outsiders"?

The forces of gentrification have reached the gates of Chinatowns. Across America, upscale property developments threaten to encroach on venerable ethnic enclaves that happen to sit on very valuable real estate. While Chinatown gentrification in some ways repeats a pattern played out in other ethnic- and minority-dominated neighborhoods, Chinatowns differentiate themselves by their symbolic importance, their history of racialization, and the ongoing transformations that embroil these spaces. Today's Chinatowns are alive with contradictions. The very "foreignness" that once forced Chinese immigrants into these self-sustaining enclaves has been repackaged to create economic value—often at the expense of the neighborhood's poorer, more vulnerable residents.

This paper will specifically examine the racial, legal, and economic underpinnings of gentrification in New York City's Chinatown. Overarching questions, however, extend well beyond the streets of lower Manhattan. What role has racial stratification played in the development of Chinatowns? How do state-sponsored economic development strategies change the makeup of Chinatowns today? What legal protections do ethnic enclaves receive? And what do they deserve? These questions lurk behind the ongoing dialogues between cities and their Chinatowns.

[...]

Land of Outsiders

Chinatowns rose out of involuntary, reflexive reactions to racial commodification.[5] Leong's premise, that America's history of "assigning value to race" underlies the racial-market paradigm, finds a potent parable in the origins of Chinatowns.[6] Prior to the mid-1800s, American society harbored an "ambivalent" view toward the Chinese.[7] Discrimination and sinophobic ideologies existed, to be sure, but records also suggest many Americans respected both the Chinese work ethic and China's standing among the world's civilizations. A California newspaper described the Chinese as "amongst the most industrious, quiet, patient people among us."[8] The governor of California declared them "one of the most worthy of our newly adopted citizens."[9] Peter Kwong and Dusanka Miscevic explain this in terms that echo Leong's theory. Until the mid-1800s, "the American racial construct had not yet assigned [the Chinese] a definite position in the social hierarchy."[10] Cheap Chinese labor pleased employers and fueled California's growing economy. But a confluence of factors, prominent among them the rise of the White labor movement, put an end to society's ambivalence about the Chinese. From the mid-1800s onward, American society assigned the Chinese a low racial value and reinforced it with overt acts of racial animus.

[…]

Chinatown's immigrants soon discovered their new neighborhood was penned in by restrictive laws designed to keep them out of mainstream society. This was the double-meaning of Chinatown—a safe haven for its inhabitants, and an enclosure. Indeed, those on the outside of Chinatowns saw them "as a way to contain a very threatening population in American life."[20] Containment—not assimilation—defined these spaces. Employment and housing discrimination made it "difficult for Chinese immigrants to find a place to live outside of Chinatown."[21] And within Chinatowns, residents lacked basic legal protections like citizenship. Overall, the cities that encircled Chinatowns ignored, or actively antagonized, their needs.

In the vacuum left by traditional government institutions, "Chinatown provided social, economic, and political mechanisms" that promoted self-sufficiency.[22] Economically, the success of Chinatown's robust ethnic enclave depended on several factors. First, Chinese employees worked for Chinese proprietors within the community. Second, Chinatowns' businesses catered to the needs of co-ethnic customers.

[…]

The neighborhood's compactness is a boon for new residents, who "rely on networks of friends and relatives and on affordable housing, food, and goods in the neighborhood."[26] Proximity also allows newcomers to locate essential social services, like doctors' offices, which was especially critical at Chinatown's formation, a time when "city governments often paid little attention to [the neighborhood's] needs."[27] For some poorer, relatively uneducated immigrants, Chinatowns provided better job prospects than the mainstream American economy.[28] One study has suggested the "ethnic network passes on valuable information that increases annual earnings by increasing the job-worker match quality and thereby the hourly wage rate, irrespective of skill level."[29] Recent immigrants' skills can yield better economic returns in Chinatowns than in the jobs available in the mainstream labor market. In that way, Chinatowns can serve as "concrete manifestations of ethnic solidarity."[30] Although economic researchers "disagree on the rate of convergence and about whether immigrants ever reach earnings parity with native workers," studies have "invariably found evidence in support of the general pattern of economic assimilation."[31]

[…]

Gentrification

Chinatown's history of racial commodification plays a major role in its rapid development today. The word many critics use to describe this development, "gentrification," brims with negative connotations: it can imply cultural sterilization, homogeneity, and displacement.[35] Typical of Chinatown's history, gentrification intertwines problems of race and economics—the process "by definition devastates the economic and racial diversity of city neighborhoods."[36] In the Urban Justice Center's definition, gentrification ties together race, displacement, and economic planning. It is "a physical, economic, and cultural process in which private developers, aided by city policies, invest in low-income and underserved neighborhoods, causing high-income people to displace low-income people, often people of color, from their homes and businesses."[37] This section will focus on the cultural costs of gentrification in Chinatowns, and specifically the consequences of racialized development on the neighborhood's longtime inhabitants. First, it is important to get a sense of how gentrification has changed the composition of Chinatown communities. Most visibly, gentrification has altered the racial and ethnic makeup of the neighborhoods. White populations in Boston, Philadelphia, and New York City's Chinatowns have grown rapidly since 2000. In New York City, the Asian and Latino populations dropped by 11 percent each from 2000 to 2010, while the White population rose by 19 percent.[38] The number of multigenerational immigrant families, too, has been dwindling as more and more young professionals move in.[39] The White newcomers to these Chinatowns generally have more money than the non-White residents they replace, another classic harbinger of gentrification. Data from New York City shows the bifurcation in process. In 2000, the median household income among Whites was $35,904, while Asian Pacific Islanders' household income was $31,368. By 2010, White median incomes in Chinatown had risen to $58,265, while the neighborhoods' Asian household incomes had dropped to $29,524.[40]

Gentrification and racial capitalism coincide when economic development depends, at least in part, on exploiting "the commodity of nonwhiteness" for value.[41] Marketing the diversity of Chinatown has in fact been part of developers' gentrification strategy.[42] Outsiders have exploited Chinatown's non-Whiteness by commodifying its racial identity to derive economic value.[43] Indeed,

Leong's article examines similar commodification in the context of college and workplace diversity. Economic development in Chinatowns takes the same tactic—diversity as a value-creating draw—and applies it to urban landscapes. But just like racial capitalism in the admissions context can do violence to an admittee's sense of identity, so, too, can racial capitalism in the gentrification context warp a community's.

Longtime residents and advocates find wry irony in the fact Chinatown's distinctive features, forged by discriminatory pressures, now "attract not only tourists to the neighborhoods' 'exotic' products and experiences, but also more affluent residents to conquer a hip and unexplored 'frontier' in city living."[44] Property developers routinely peddle the neighborhood's "authenticity" as a way to lure more affluent residents into the area, who will pay higher rents than existing tenants. "Nonwhiteness," to use Leong's racial-capitalist framework, "has therefore become something desirable—and for many, it has become a commodity to be pursued, captured, possessed, and used."[45] For example:

> "Chinatown is a sensory experience. People pushing past stalls of fresh produce on crowded streets. Exotic-looking vegetables and fruits accompany Florida oranges."
>
> "New York's Chinatown represents a thick slice of foreign culture dropped directly into the socio-ethnic stew that is Manhattan ... Chinatown's Blade Runner ambience and still-exotic charm reinforced its appeal."
>
> "It's unclear how much someone who can afford a $2 million pad will enjoy the one-of-a-kind bodegas-cum-mini-groceries that stock frozen squid snacks."[46]

[...]

The relationship between gentrification and racial capitalism has thus been fueled, in part, by the media and real estate industries, which advance the idea of Chinatown "as an exotic yet chic neighborhood on the cusp of a major transformation."[51]

[...]

At any rate, the cultural value featured in Chinatown's marketing seems oriented outward. Depicting Chinatown as an exotic frontier, tinged with adventure, seems designed to lure "hip" New Yorkers into the neighborhood rather than to forge relationships within the community. And the marketing, it must be said, often works. During the first wave of Chinatown gentrification in the 1980s, for example, one new resident explained to the *New York Times,* "It's the best all-round deal for my money, because it's beautiful and peaceful and you can smell spices all over."[59] As a *Time Out* excerpt observes, the wealthier newcomers do not seem poised to mix into Chinatown's "socio-ethnic stew."[60] Chinatown locals, again, appear more like "passive emblems," rather than full-standing neighbors.

The other type of cultural harm caused by Chinatown's gentrification goes to economics. The marketing push surrounding gentrification allows development projects to draw economic value from Chinatown's non-Whiteness without ensuring Chinatown itself benefits from the bargain. Property developers and brokers capitalize on Chinatown's non-Whiteness—using bywords such as "exotic" and "foreign"—to generate higher rents and greater economic value. But for whom? Critics point out Chinatown's existing residents cannot consume the high-end goods and services ushered in by new businesses. According to a 2013 survey by AALDEF, median income in the New York's Chinatown area is $36,899, "with 27 percent of residents making below $16,556."[61] Similarly, new development could push out Chinatowns' small businesses, the lifeblood of the community's exotic charm. A 2008 survey found almost half (48 percent) of small-business proprietors in Chinatown considered relocating out of Chinatown or shutting down altogether.[62] Such incongruity between the economic influx and the existing inhabitants suggests economic value may not inure to the benefit of Chinatown's poorer and more vulnerable residents.

To be sure, "economic development" writ large carries with it both harmful and beneficial consequences. Gentrification can lead to displacement, but it can also lower crime rates, broaden the tax base, and bolster public finances.[63] Indeed, discussing gentrification by solely fixating on its positive or negative aspects risks creating a false dichotomy between unbridled growth and no development. Chinatowns can benefit, of course, from economic growth. Its housing stock, small business revenues, and employee wage rates could all use improvement. But what Chinatown's supporters demand is growth that fairly accommodates the existing population.

[...]

Conclusion

Unlike counterparts in other major American cities, the fears of an "ethnic theme park" have not yet been realized in lower Manhattan.[118] The preeminence of New York's Chinatown among satellite Chinese-American communities has allowed it to become a cultural hub, with spokes reaching out to many different neighborhoods. Chinatown's survival today hinges on characteristics that have shaped it throughout its history: expansive co-ethnic networks, self-sufficiency, and a genius for reinvention. But from its origins as a refuge for Chinese immigrants facing discrimination, the neighborhood has been defined by the actions and interests of outsiders. Today, that pattern continues as ordinary Chinatown inhabitants get little say in the character, direction, and pace of economic development in the area. While gentrification can ultimately benefit Chinatown, rudderless development policies ignore the historical fact that "Chinatowns were products of extreme forms of racial segregation."[119] Going forward, a conception of property rights that recognizes community rights may better balance the needs of Chinatown with the expansion of the cities around it.

Notes

[5] Kwong, Peter, *The New Chinatown* (New York: Hill and Wang, 1996): 13.

[6] Leong, supra note 1.

[7] Kwong, Peter, and Dušanka Miščević, *Chinese America: The Untold Story of America's Oldest New Community* (New York: The New Press, 2005): 50.

[8] Ibid, 43–44.

[9] Ibid, 44.

[10] Ibid.

[20] Goyette, supra note 15.

[21] Ibid.

[22] Bock, Deborah Lyn, "The Historical Function of Chinatown and Its Application to Philadelphia," master's thesis (Philadelphia: University of Pennsylvania, 1976): 42.

[26] "Chinatown," supra note 23.

[27] Ibid, 7; Li, supra note 24.

[28] Highly educated, highly skilled immigrants usually transition directly into the mainstream economy, without resort to an ethnic enclave economy.

[29] Damm, Anna Piil, "Ethnic Enclaves and Immigrant Labor Market Outcomes: Quasi-Experimental Evidence," *Journal of Labor Economics* Vol. 27, No. 2 (Chicago: University of Chicago Press, 2009): 27.

[30] Xie, Yu, and Margaret Gough, "Ethnic Enclaves and the Earnings of Immigrants," *Demography* Vol. 48, No. 4 (New York: Springer, 2011): 1297.

[31] Ibid, 1295.

[35] See Weinstein, Hannah, "Fighting for a Place Called Home: Litigation Strategies for Challenging Gentrification," *UCLA Law Review* Vol. 62, No. 3 (Los Angeles: UCLA School of Law, 2015): 794–832.

[36] Ibid, 797.

[37] "Converting Chinatown: A Snapshot of a Neighborhood Becoming Unaffordable and Unlivable," The Urban Justice Center, 2008.

[38] "Chinatown," supra note 23.

[39] Ibid.

[40] Ibid.

[41] Leong, supra note 1.

[42] "Converting Chinatown," supra note 37.

[43] I use the term "outsiders" rather than "Whites" to avoid oversimplifying the relationship between Chinatowns and the wider world. Certainly, Whites led nineteenth century campaigns to expel and exclude the Chinese. But the White/non-White binary cannot fully describe the narrative of gentrification. Chinese bosses exploit co-ethnic employees, Chinese landlords harass co-ethnic tenants, and Asian financing has at times hastened Asian American displacement. "Outsider" represents the idea that those in power—White, Asian, or other—exploit those without it. The dynamic still conforms to Leong's theory. What characterizes racial capitalism, after all, is the notion that others can gain from one's own racial identity.

[44] "Converting Chinatown," supra note 37.

[45] Leong, "Racial Capitalism," 2155.

[46] "Converting Chinatown," supra note 37.

[51] Ibid.

[59] Howe, Marvine, "Have-Nots Fear 'Manhattanization' as Developers Size Up Chinatown," *The New York Times*, 21 September 1984.

[60] "Converting Chinatown," supra note 37.

[61] "Chinatown," supra note 23.

[62] Ibid.

[63] See Byrne, J., "Two Cheers for Gentrification," *Howard Law Journal* Vol. 46 (Washington, DC: Howard University Press, Spring 2003): 405–432. Even Byrne's essay, however, which praises the effects of gentrification on communities as well as low-income populations, acknowledges "the persistent failure of government[s] to produce or secure affordable housing."

[118] Tabor, Nick, "How Has Chinatown Stayed Chinatown?," *New York Magazine*, 24 September 2015.

[119] Goyette, supra note 15.

> "Ultimately, gentrification plays
> a small role in the ebb and flow
> of neighborhood social and
> cultural life."

Historic Neighborhoods Evoke Strong Emotions

Charles William Lawrence

In the following excerpted viewpoint, Charles William Lawrence argues that gentrification can be a positive process, particularly concerning the emotional issue of historic preservation. Ultimately, the author recognizes that gentrification is part of the "ebb and flow" of the life of neighborhoods, with positive and negative elements, but should not be considered as always being a destructive process. Lawrence earned a master's degree in historic preservation from the University of Pennsylvania.

As you read, consider the following questions:

1. What are some of the positive outcomes of gentrification?
2. What are some of the negative outcomes of gentrification?
3. What is meant by the "ebb and flow" of a neighborhood?

"New Neighbors in Old Neighborhoods: Explaining the Role of Heritage Conservation in Sociocultural Sustainability and Gentrification," by Charles William Lawrence, University of Pennsylvania, 2010. Reprinted by permission.

The term *gentrification* was coined in 1964 when Ruth Glass wrote about the demographic shift taking place in some of London's working-class neighborhoods:

> One by one, many of the working-class quarters of London have been invaded by the middle classes upper and lower. Shabby, modest mews and cottages—two rooms up and two down— have been taken over, when their leases have expired, and have become elegant, expensive residences … Once this process of "gentrification" starts in a district it goes on rapidly until all or most of the original working class occupiers are displaced and the whole social character of the district is changed. (Glass, 1964)

Gentrification is produced by two interrelated processes: the class-based recolonization of residential neighborhoods and a reinvestment in the physical building stock (Atkinson, 2003). The resultant increases in housing values and rents leads to the displacement of some current residents, often renters and those with low cash flow (i.e. the elderly and unemployed), and the exclusion of new low-income households. Thus, the neighborhood changes from a lower-class to a higher-class use with businesses and services following suit. Ultimately, the preexisting social and cultural systems of the neighborhood are replaced by new ones. The loss of residents and of familiar social and cultural systems is at the core of the gentrification issue. The high visibility of physical upgrading and in some cases, of heritage conservation within the process of gentrification makes it difficult to disentangle from the negative sociocultural side effects of displacement and loss of character.

Effects of Gentrification

> The crucial point about gentrification is that it involves not only a social change but also, at the neighborhood scale, a physical change in the housing stock and an economic change in the land and housing market. It is this combination of social, physical, and economic change that distinguishes gentrification as an identifiable process/set of processes. (Smith, 1987)

Far from being a completely negative process, gentrification can bring with it several positive outcomes: reinvestment, increased levels of home ownership, improved public services, improved commercial activities, renovation of vacant and abandoned properties, adaptive use of "white elephant" structures, increased property tax, sales tax, and income tax revenues, neighborhood jobs, property value appreciation, and economic integration (Rypkema D. D., 2004). Yet it is the negative outcomes that make gentrification such a polarizing topic; rising housing costs, changes in the human character of the neighborhood, loss of a sense of "power" and "ownership" by long-term residents, and potential conflicts between new residents and long-term residents (Rypkema D. D., 2004).

There is debate among scholars over whether gentrification is a "net positive" process or if that view represents a "tyranny of the statistical majority" (Newman & Wyly, 2006). A sophisticated understanding of the distribution of the costs and benefits is needed in order to determine how gentrification affects different segments of society. For the cities in which gentrification occurs, the reinvestment in neighborhoods brings substantial benefits with minimal costs; increased tax base, new investment, and a better image contrasted with minimal relocation costs. For incoming residents gentrification affords them relatively cheaper housing in a desirable neighborhood close to their workplace. For pre-existing homeowners, gentrification offers the possibility of substantial profits from the sale of their house but this often comes with a feeling of regret at leaving their old neighborhood behind. For non-home owning residents, gentrification threatens their way of life. Increasing costs and changes in the social and cultural character of the neighborhood inflame the passions of many long-time residents. However, enhancements in neighborhood safety, services and amenities are often regarded as acceptable tradeoffs for the increased costs and changes in character. For some residents gentrification leads to displacement due to unmanageable increases in housing costs; though a statistically small group, the displaced have become central to the gentrification debate.

Causal Models of Gentrification

Early efforts to understand gentrification began in earnest in the mid-1970s through the mid-to-late-1980s. In an analysis of these studies London, et al. (1986) organize the explanatory factors into several categories; demographic, ecological, sociological, and political-economic. Demographic factors include the change in population compositions that lead to resettlement of inner-city neighborhoods; aspects like the "unprecedented number of young adults" coming to age in the baby boom generation. Other aspects include populations that are waiting longer to marry and have children, more women in the workforce, and an increased number of dual-wage households. These demographic trends create a greater number of risk-tolerant pioneers willing to settle in transitional neighborhoods (Schaffer & Smith, 1986).

Gentrification's ecological causes stem from land-use changes from manufacturing to white-collar, technology-based industry. The implication is that as heavy industry is decentralized, the central business district shifts its focus to white collar labor which in turn attracts new residents to the inner-city residential ring, previously housing the working-class labor force dependant on the now-absent factories.

The sociological explanation posits that a greater number of the population is shifting from a rural ideal to a pro-urban mentality. These urbanites move into the city (or, as the case may be, move within the city) seeking the cultural and recreational amenities associated with city life. London, et al. (1986) propose that the restoration of historic buildings falls under this sociological factor, as it may represent an act of self-expression or be a part of larger nostalgic national trends (such as the 1976 Bicentennial).

The political-economic factor of gentrification is the most widely debated area of scholarship. It centers on issues of supply-

and-demand, market efficiency, and the distribution of costs and benefits. Traditionalists view factors such as rising housing costs, rising transportation costs, availability of urban land, and desegregation as determinants of gentrification. The Marxist camp views the political-economic factors as being intentionally produced, or, at the least, impossible to avoid; policies of neglect and disinvestment that lead to blight and ultimately to clearance and renewal.

According to Neil Smith, the person most associated with the Marxist camp, the process of devalorization happens through "the movement of capital from the cities to the suburbs; the shift towards a higher level of rental property; potential blockbusting which occurs when real estate professionals purchase homes at a low cost and then sell them to minorities at a substantial markup; redlining which occurs when private banks and funding institutions cease to provide mortgages to individuals living in certain neighborhoods; and the abandonment of inner city dwellings" (Smith, 1996).

The result of this is what Smith calls the "rent gap," the difference between "the actual capitalized ground rent of a plot of land given its present use and the potential ground rent that might be gleaned under a 'higher and better' use" (Smith, 1987). "When this gap grows sufficiently large, rehabilitation (or for that matter, renewal) can begin to challenge the rates of return available elsewhere and capital flows back" (Smith, 1979).

Ultimately, several conditions come together to produce gentrification; within the neighborhood, a tight housing market with the conditions outlined in Smith's arguments; within the city's commercial district, an increase in job growth; outside of the city core, an increase in traffic and congestion (or a general reduction in quality of life); within the policy arena, tax incentives and revitalization programs; and within the social arena, a renewed preference for urban amenities (Kennedy & Leonard, 2001). Hamnett simplifies the conditions further, breaking the causes of gentrification into three criteria; supply of gentrifiable property, supply of potential gentrifiers, and demand for inner-city living (Hamnett, The Blind Men and the Elephant: The Explanation of Gentrification, 1991).

Different degrees of each criterion will result in a different sort of change; the building stock changes, the people change, and the sense of place changes—these changes do not necessarily always lead to gentrification. This may occur according to cyclic process of urban succession (White, 1984), the more-or-less predictable replacement of one community with another—whether speaking in ecological, sociological or economic terms.

Part of this process of change can be explained through an examination of the shift in the modes of production in a city and the increasing availability of suburban living. Beginning with the development of light rail and followed by the automobile, suburban life became a reality to more and more people who could afford it. Cheaper property and ease of access not only attracted white-collar residents, it also attracted industry. As industry left cities for suburbs, so too did the majority of the employable working-class population and their families. In their places, came successive waves of in-migrant populations that took advantage of the surplus of affordable housing, much of it only available as rentals. However, the continued loss of employers, lack of new investment, racist housing policies, and macroeconomic troubles took their toll on cities; populations continued to decline and neighborhoods deteriorated.

On a very small scale, middle-class urban "pioneers" looking for distinctive neighborhoods close to the central business district began to move in to these deteriorated neighborhoods—finding affordable housing, urban amenities, and distinctive building stock. City governments also began to use planning tools to re-imagine their policies and reshape the urban landscape, often in the shape of urban renewal and slum clearance schemes. Schaffer and Smith (1986) point out, however, that the processes behind gentrification have been noted since the 19th century; alternatively called "the improvements" by the English or embourgeoisement in response to Haussmann's plan for Paris (1852–1870).

Throughout the latter-half of the 20th century, cities have worked desperately to revive their cores, using a multitude of policies and tools. Urban resettlement, however, still plays a proportionately small role in overall urban population patterns that have been consistently declining since the 1950s—while suburban areas have conversely increased in population. Only in the most recent urban demographic data analyses have urban population declines shown a slowdown and in a few cases a reverse.[1]

Dennis Gale (1980), exploring further the prior work of Phillip Clay (1979), suggests that this "resettlement" of neighborhoods occurs in stages rather than being specific to the latter half of the 20th century. In stage one, "a few 'risk-oblivious' households purchase older housing." In stage two, "the local media and a few real estate concerns 'discover' the resettlement neighborhood" and "risk-prone" buyers move in. In stage three, after several years, a middle-class presence has been established and "risk-averse" buyers appear. This model can be applied to any gentrifying neighborhood at any given time—regardless of larger population movements. This totalizing ecological stage model is not unlike Smith's totalizing political-economic model in which individuals and culture are given little agency over the forces at play in gentrification.

The most recent research has challenged traditional models by presenting several alternative forms of gentrification. These include marginal gentrification, upgrading, and incumbent upgrading. Marginal gentrification occurs when the incoming residents have more "cultural capital than economic capital," resulting in a change in neighborhood character without the associated increase in income levels or property values. Upgrading refers to a change from middle-class to upper-class, much in the same way that traditional gentrification occurs. Incumbent upgrading occurs when long-term residents engage in an internal process of rehabilitation and revitalization with very little change in residents.

Tourism gentrification (the conversion of housing to short-term "vacation" rentals) and super-gentrification (the displacement of the middle- and upper-classes by the ultra-wealthy) have also been discussed (Bures & Cain, 2008).

Significance and Extent of Gentrification

The many different causal models for gentrification and the several alternative forms presented in recent scholarship tend to muddy the intellectual waters surrounding the already complex issue. They also illustrate how the physical rehabilitation of neighborhoods can result in several different scenarios that do not necessarily lead to displacement or drastic sociocultural change. In fact, a recent study done by Lance Freeman and Frank Braconi (2004) in New York indicates that large scale displacement may not actually occur any more in "gentrifying" neighborhoods than other neighborhoods. Another recent study, published by the National Bureau of Economic Research (NBER), found that not only were long-term residents not moving out of "gentrifying" neighborhoods, they were experiencing widespread increases in income (McKinnish, Walsh, & White, 2008). However, another study found that while low-income households were not more likely to move from gentrifying neighborhoods they did experience an increase in housing costs without an increase in income (Vigdor, Massey, & Rivlin, 2002).

Several studies have shown that on average urban populations move once every five to seven years (or 15–20% of the urban population moves every year). Of these, in gentrifying neighborhoods, about 23% of the outmovers would fall into the category of displacement depending on how that term is defined[2] and only 17% of those are adversely affected (Schill & Nathan, 1983). That means in a neighborhood of 10,000 one can expect on average 1,500 to 2,000 people to move in or out each year with about 400 of those people having been displaced and less than 100 worse off. Schill and Nathan's results have been heavily criticized for their restricted definition of gentrification and an insufficient methodology, yet there are few other studies that have attempted to quantify displacement to this extent and those that do have not had markedly different results.[3]

In another study, Jacob Vigdor (2002) asks "does gentrification harm the poor?" After a very thorough analysis he concludes that there is not one outcome but several caused by two separate mechanisms. In one scenario, the poor are adversely affected by larger changes in income distribution and property values. In the other scenario, as some inner city neighborhoods become desirable and more people move in, the current poor residents must make a rational decision to move and accept the cost of relocating, but perhaps enjoy better housing elsewhere, or stay and accept the increased costs (economic and cultural), but enjoy better services and opportunities. Hamnett even concludes that displacement and sociocultural change take place "largely as a result of long-term industrial and occupational change, not of gentrification per se" (Hamnett, 2003). Research continues to show that gentrification is neither a continually progressive process nor that it has a single outcome or end-point (Gotham, 2005).

Ultimately, gentrification plays a small role in the ebb and flow of neighborhood social and cultural life. However, the forces behind gentrification (housing markets, demographics, and sociocultural trends) can result in an imbalance of costs and benefits that harms the least advantaged in a community while rewarding those able to take advantage of the changes. These forces also play a role in the conservation of the historic built environment and can result in the loss of some buildings and the rehabilitation of others. It is important to understand the role conservation can play in mitigating these negative effects for both a community and their buildings.

[...]

Final Words

The historic built environment has an incredible ability to evoke strong emotions. For many, the built environment holds memories, cultural meaning, and a sense of place in the world. However, no place is frozen in time and investment and divestment, both economically and socioculturally, change a place over time. The role of heritage conservation is to work within that context of change to find ways to preserve valued places while maintaining and enhancing other contemporary values. In a word, heritage conservation endeavors to make the historic built environment relevant.

Often, the question is asked; "Whose history is to be conserved, whose values are being protected?" These are tough questions with no easy answers. But the best answer may be "Yours." Values-based heritage conservation seeks to evaluate and assess historic assets and match them with contemporary needs. Good conservation programs start with the community and work outwards. The goal of heritage conservation is to project the past into the future and the only way this is done successfully is by seeking triple-bottom line sustainability in values-based conservation planning.

Notes

1. See, for example, recent census data for Washington DC and Philadelphia located in the appendices.

2. Peter Marcuse goes so far as to say that displacement can be preemptive, whereby "housing opportunities of lower-income households are restricted," forcing these residents to look elsewhere for housing, producing what he calls "exclusionary displacement" (Marcuse, 1986).

3. For the criticism of Schill and Nathan see Smith and DeBres (1984). Other studies quantifying displacement include Newman & Wyly (2006), Freeman and Braconi (2004), Vigdor (2002) and Freeman (2005).

| "Fresh thinking is needed to devise targeted, sustained efforts to … further the economic revitalization of blighted urban neighborhoods."

Gentrifiers Prefer Neighborhoods That Are Already White

Jackelyn Hwang

In the following viewpoint, Jackelyn Hwang argues that gentrification does not affect minority neighborhoods in the way that many believe it does. The author contends that gentrifiers are more likely to move to white neighborhoods. Depending on the racial makeup of the community, gentrifiers may be more or less likely to take a chance on a neighborhood, which explains the high levels of inequality and poverty found in many urban areas. The author seeks to understand these trends by exploring how gentrification occurs, where it occurs and is less likely to occur, and what this inequality means in terms of creating urban policies. Hwang is an assistant professor of sociology at Stanford University.

"How 'Gentrification' in American Cities Maintains Racial Inequality and Segregation," by Jackelyn Hwang, Scholars Strategy Network, August 2014. http://www. scholarsstrategynetwork.org/brief/how-gentrification-american-cities-maintains-racial-inequality-and-segregation. Licensed under CC BY-ND 4.0 International.

As you read, consider the following questions:

1. What are the two contradictory trends that the author mentions?
2. What effects do ethnic minorities have on the potential for a neighborhood's gentrification?
3. How does gentrification actually perpetuate racial segregation and inequality?

After decades of population declines, cities are adding population more rapidly than suburbs for the first time in nearly a century, as trendy middle-class neighborhoods continue to grow in number and size across areas that more affluent Americans once considered places to avoid. Yet research tells us that American cities continue to exhibit high levels of neighborhood inequality and poverty, especially for racial minorities. My research seeks to understand these two seemingly contradictory trends by examining how gentrification unfolds over time. Do neighborhoods gentrify at the same pace or to the same degree? Does gentrification spread evenly into its adjacent disinvested neighborhoods? If not, what factors influence these differences—leaving some urban areas mired in extreme poverty?

My research with sociologist and SSN Scholar Robert Sampson examined these issues in a study of Chicago neighborhoods. We define gentrification as the reinvestment and renewal of previously debilitated urban neighborhoods that occurs as middle- and upper-middle-class residents move in. To measure neighborhood change, we went beyond traditional sources of Census data to use information on the location of institutions and urban amenities, police data, community surveys, and—most innovative of all— visual information from Google Street View. The visible streetscape of neighborhoods provides direct indicators of change, such as new construction, rehabilitation, and beautification efforts. By assessing the presence of our various indicators of gentrification for nearly

2,000 blocks, we were able to measure degrees of gentrification for neighborhoods of varying racial composition. Additional research I have done also probes the impact of immigration.

Minority Neighborhoods Are Not Readily Gentrified

Neighborhood selection is an important reason that poor enclaves and racial segregation persist in US cities. Racial and ethnic stereotypes influence people's choices about where they want to live and which neighborhoods to avoid—and people also consider crime, property values, school quality, and local amenities. In popular media and political debates, gentrification is often depicted as a process in which middle-class whites move into and thus integrate minority neighborhoods. But in fact, gentrifiers prefer already white neighborhoods; they are least attracted to black neighborhoods and see Asian and Latino neighborhoods as middling options.

We analyzed shifts over time in or near debilitated Chicago neighborhoods that had showed signs of gentrification in 1995. Race and neighborhood reputations turned out to play an important role, as gentrification proceeded more slowly through 2009 in areas with higher shares of blacks and Latinos. Even after we took into account other important factors such as crime, poverty, and proximity to amenities, neighborhoods with more blacks and Latinos were less likely to continue to gentrify or even to reverse course and decline after early signs of transformation. Gentrification also tends to slow down in the face of perceptions of disorder in a neighborhood, even if the actual level of disorder does not match perceptions.

Sometimes gentrification does affect areas with racial and ethnic diversity, but we saw little such change in Chicago neighborhoods where more than forty percent of residents were black. Only neighborhoods that were at least 35 percent white continued to gentrify after 1995.

GENTRIFICATION AND TRENDS

No discussion on urban revitalization is complete without addressing the issue of gentrification. This byproduct of redevelopment has proven to be a persistent source of tension between new and old inhabitants of urban communities throughout the country.

Much of the impetus for these trends arises from local government policies and private developers who target development in communities to attract new residents to a city. From 2000–2010, this was the case in Washington, DC when Mayor Anthony Williams's investments in higher-end amenities in previously neglected neighborhoods resulted in an increase of 30,000 residents after five consecutive decades of population loss.

Researcher Lisa Sturtevant examines the gentrification that resulted from this policy. Sturtevant is interested primarily in the characteristics of those moving in and out of the city and the broader regional affects of gentrification.

The study finds that a significantly greater number of households from the ages of 18–24 moved into the city than moved out and that most of these were single-person households. In terms of race, 53.7 percent of new migrants are white, a significantly higher number than non-movers, out-migrants, and within-city movers, while 41.4 percent of out-migrants are African-American, compared

The Impact of Asian and Latino Immigration

Immigration has increased sharply in recent decades, shifting the ethnic and racial composition of many urban neighborhoods— sometimes boosting housing demand and creating new local businesses. To look at immigration and gentrification, I tracked demographic and socioeconomic changes since the 1970s in economically struggling neighborhoods identified in 23 large US cities. Tellingly, the neighborhoods that gentrified were overwhelmingly multiethnic in the 1970s, and remained relatively diverse over the next few decades. But the ethnic specifics mattered. An early presence of Asians and rising proportions of Asian with 26.1 percent of in-migrants. Whereas higher income white households are more likely to stay within the city, higher income black households are more likely to leave than those with lower incomes. Further, black households with higher educational attainment are significantly more likely to leave the geographic region altogether. Overall, Sturtevant finds evidence of displacement in the significantly higher likelihood that those who moved out of the District of Columbia were from lower income and less educated households.

The study also finds familiar patterns in the migration behavior of new residents: residents arrive as young singles and leave when they become married and have children. The transience of new residents complicates plans for sustained urban population growth, while the socioeconomic characteristics of those coming and going show evidence of reinforcing residential segregation, particularly as black households that remain in the region are increasingly those that are lower-educated and less skilled.

As the case in DC demonstrates, successful revitalization plans may not necessarily translate into improved quality of life for a city's residents and may in fact drive the residents most in need of assistance to leave the city altogether.

"District of Change: Gentrification and Demographic Trends in Washington, DC," by Corey Chan, *Chicago Policy Review*, July 23, 2014.

residents tended to be positively associated with gentrification, while the same was not true for a growing Hispanic presence. Contrasts were stronger when blacks were a major presence. What is more, in cities where Hispanics had a well-established presence, economically distressed neighborhoods continued to struggle as more Hispanics moved in.

Consider Seattle compared to Chicago. Seattle had a much less diverse population and has only recently become an immigrant destination, while Chicago has served as a major gateway for many decades, particularly for Latinos who make up nearly one-third of its population. Data for Chicago neighborhoods reveal that

Latino neighborhoods have experienced little or slowed rates of gentrification. But in Seattle, influxes of immigrants, often Asians, have furthered neighborhood gentrification.

Implications for Racial Inequality and Urban Policy

In sum, gentrification in US cities has been problematic for low-income minorities, and not just because new middle-class residents displace poor people. Despite gentrification in some locales, economically blighted black neighborhoods, plus those with growing Hispanic populations, have tended to remain disadvantaged. Some neighborhoods that attracted Asian immigrants experienced ethnic diversification along with gentrification, but the arrival of more Latinos has gone hand in hand with gentrification only in cities where Latinos are not already negatively stigmatized.

In many of America's cities, civic leaders have pinned hopes for urban revitalization on gentrification and efforts to attract immigrants. But facts on the ground show that they need to weigh the probability that these forms of urban change can further isolate poor blacks and Latinos and—contrary to media claims—actually increase racial segregation and inequality. Urban policymakers should take note: Fresh thinking is needed to devise targeted, sustained efforts to protect minorities from displacement, ensure affordable housing for those with low incomes, and further the economic revitalization of blighted urban neighborhoods. Gentrification and immigration are not panaceas.

Periodical and Internet Sources Bibliography

The following articles have been selected to supplement the diverse views presented in this chapter.

Josh Green, "How Gentrification Really Changes a Neighborhood," *Atlanta*, March 2016. http://www.atlantamagazine.com /homeandgarden/the-gentrifier/.

Jackelyn Hwang, "The Social Construction of a Gentrifying Neighborhood," *Urban Affairs Review*, March 2, 2015. http:// journals.sagepub.com/doi/full/10.1177/1078087415570643.

Charles F. McElwee III, "When Historic Preservation Depends on Gentrification," *American Conservative*, July 7, 2017. http:// www.theamericanconservative.com/urbs/historic-preservation -gentrification-urbanism/.

Tanvi Misra, "Gentrification Doesn't Mean Diversity," *CityLab*, May 15, 2017. https://www.citylab.com/equity/2017/05/gentrifying -neighborhoods-arent-really-diverse/526092/.

Shelterforce, "The Cultural Ramifications of Gentrification in New Orleans," August 23, 2017. https://shelterforce.org/2017/08/23 /cultural-ramifications-gentrification-new-orleans/.

Dianne Solis, "To Ease Gentrification Pain, Some Latinos Embrace 'Gentefication' to Preserve Culture," *Chicago Tribune*, February 14, 2018. http://www.chicagotribune.com/voiceit/ct-hoy-to-ease -gentrification-pain-some-latinos-embrace-gentefication-to -preserve-culture-20180214-story.html.

Willy Staley, "When 'Gentrification' Isn't About Housing," *New York Times Magazine*, January 23, 2018. https://www.nytimes.com /2018/01/23/magazine/when-gentrification-isnt-about-housing .html.

Rebecca Summer, "Black Branding and Gentrification in Washington, D.C.," *Edge Effects*, May 23, 2017. http://edgeeffects.net/cappucino -city/.

CHAPTER 4

Does Gentrification Have Economic Benefits?

Chapter Preface

One of the most frequent arguments concerning gentrification has to do with whether it is economically beneficial, both for the original neighborhood and its residents and for newcomers. Many people believe that gentrification can only have negative effects on lower-income residents of a neighborhood, because of rising rents and costs of living. Basic grocery stores and family restaurants may be displaced by designer coffee chains and organic markets, which are often economically out of the reach of low-income families. It is also argued that employment opportunities maybe decreased as well, if long-established businesses are forced to leave the area.

However, there are also studies that show that gentrification can be an economic advantage for poorer residents when their neighborhoods become more upscale. Many are shown to enjoy an increase in credit scores and income. Homeowners usually see their property values rise. There may be more jobs available in new businesses. In addition, as property tax rates rise and bring in more revenue, the community benefits economically as a whole, with more money for schools and public services as well as public safety net programs like rent assistance. Also, developers may be required by city policies to build a certain amount of subsidized housing for every upscale, luxury development they create, which makes more low-income housing available to residents.

Experts stress that every city and every situation is different, and while gentrification is not always economically damaging for a neighborhood's original residents, there are cases where it does push people out of affordable housing and force them to move to other areas. It often depends on the economic status of the city as a whole. As with any issue that raises emotions in those involved, it depends on every neighborhood's particular makeup and situation as to whether gentrification will be economically good or bad.

> *"Gentrification is about redevelopment that benefits one class of people by unfortunately sending another class packing."*

Everyone Can Benefit from Gentrification with Equitable Development

Beth McConnell

In the following viewpoint, Beth McConnell argues that gentrification is the process of redevelopment that benefits one class of people while forcing the other class to leave. The author sees the process of equitable development as being a way to ensure that neighborhoods are equally developed, not just those that are gentrified, but all parts of the city. She stresses that development should be about people as well as real estate. McConnell is policy director of the Philadelphia Association of Community Development Corporations.

As you read, consider the following questions:

1. What is equitable development?
2. What is the author's overall attitude about gentrification in this city?
3. What specific suggestions does she have to create an equitable development platform for Philadelphia?

"Equitable Development: The Answer to Gentrification; Advancing Equitable Development Is Critical to Philadelphia's Economic Recovery," by Beth McConnell, *Social Innovations Journal*, January 27, 2016. Reprinted by permission.

I can't walk through Center City Philadelphia these days without having to cross the street several times to avoid construction projects. A twenty-six-story residential and commercial venture is rising from a former parking lot in between my morning coffee stop and the office, and in every other direction, brand new high-end apartments, condos, hotels, restaurants and retail are rising too. I don't mind the extra steps; it's good exercise for me and a great investment for the city. But the development boom that started in Center City, and is now spreading to surrounding neighborhoods like Point Breeze, Fishtown, Francisville and others with homes that are now selling at $400k or higher, and nationally recognized restaurants with pricey menus opening up on neighborhood commercial corridors, is like any other form of pressure: it pushes other entities away. When those entities are people and their small businesses, we've got gentrification.

Gentrification is about redevelopment that benefits one class of people by unfortunately sending another class packing. They may no longer be able to keep up with rising rents for their small business or apartment. Their limited incomes may not be able to absorb an increase in property taxes as a result of higher real estate assessments. Sometimes, gentrification can occur when affordable goods or services can no longer be found in a neighborhood, causing lower income residents to move.

Why should people who are interested in a stronger, healthier Philadelphia care? After all, people move all the time, and businesses come and go for a lot of reasons. But when they are pushed out of improving communities, we all lose.

A recent report from the Federal Reserve Bank of Philadelphia[1] used credit report data to track how people moved in and out of gentrifying neighborhoods in Philadelphia. Their research showed that when lower credit score residents (who are likely lower-income) move out of gentrifying neighborhoods, they move to neighborhoods with poorer quality of life, with lower performing schools, higher crime rates, and/or higher unemployment rates. When they were able to stay in the improving neighborhood, however; their credit scores actually boosted by an average of 11 points, a proxy for improvement in their financial health. Research[2] shows that poor children who grow up in good neighborhoods have a much better chance of breaking generational cycles of poverty and becoming economically mobile later in life. So if we want to attack Philadelphia's stubbornly high poverty rate, we must ensure that low-income people can stay in—or choose to move to—good quality neighborhoods.

When small businesses are displaced from a neighborhood, this can mean the end to the business, not just a relocation. Businesses that rely on foot-traffic or being easily accessible to public transit may not be able to survive if they are pushed out of the storefront in which they've figured out how to operate. That means families lose their jobs and incomes, and neighborhood residents lose access to the affordable goods and services that they provided. Alternatively, if we had tools to help those businesses stay in improving neighborhoods and benefit from the changes, their revenues could rise and provide even greater economic opportunity to their families and the city.

Meanwhile, what's happening to the neighborhoods that are not gentrifying? They continue to struggle with high rates of poverty, vacancy, blight and crime. Their residents aren't any better off for that multimillion-dollar development downtown, which they probably subsidized with a tax abatement or other form of public funds. Responses to gentrification should also include responses to neighborhoods that continue to be disinvested.

The answer to these challenges—and the answer to gentrification—is not less investment from the private sector. It's more investment in the people and places that the private market is not serving, so that they can stay in improving communities or choose to move to good neighborhoods, and see their own struggling neighborhood get better. Because Philadelphia does better when we all do better, now is the time to advance policies that will leverage the positive changes occurring in some of our neighborhoods for the benefit of those who would otherwise be left out. That is Equitable Development.

To advance Equitable Development, the Philadelphia Association of Community Development Corporations (PACDC), which represents organizations that work to revitalize neighborhoods and improve the quality of life for Philadelphians, released "Beyond Gentrification, Toward Equitable Neighborhoods: An Equitable Development Policy Platform for Philadelphia." The Platform contains nineteen recommendations in five key areas that Mayor Kenney and City Council should advance:

1. Strengthen the Ability of Neighborhood Groups and Residents to Create Inclusive Communities

Strong neighborhoods are made up of neighbors who care about their communities and welcome new residents, as well as community-based organizations that provide a forum for input and action to create inclusive neighborhoods. Through the Philadelphia City Planning Commission's Citizens Planning Institute, community residents should be given the knowledge and tools to participate in the Registered Community Organization (RCO) process and other planning and zoning decisions in effective, inclusive ways. Nonprofit community, civic and neighborhood associations play a vital role in engaging neighborhood residents and connecting them to vital services and programs, yet are vastly under-resourced. The City should boost to $4 million per year its investment in Neighborhood Advisory Committees (NACs) and other neighborhood-based groups that engage the community. Market-rate development projects that receive public subsidies should be required to advance Equitable Development in a meaningful way, such as through a setting aside of affordable residential or commercial spaces.

2. Create and Preserve Quality, Affordable Home Choices in Every Part of the City

Housing policies are a significant way we can attack economic segregation in Philadelphia. The Kenney Administration must lead by creating a comprehensive housing strategy to address our city's needs for quality affordable homes, including at least doubling dedicated funding for the Philadelphia Housing Trust Fund to $25 million per year. We must boost strategies to end homelessness, build and preserve more affordable homeownership and rental homes in every part of the city, including homes that are permanently affordable, spur more market-rate development, and ensure that residents are not involuntarily displaced from the neighborhoods that they call home. It's time to review the 10-Year Property Tax Abatement to determine if it must be updated for our current real estate market.

3. Expand Economic Opportunities on Our Neighborhood Corridors and Increase Local Hiring and Sourcing by Major Employers and Developers

If Center City is the heart of commerce in Philadelphia, our neighborhood commercial corridors are its economic veins. Funding for programs to improve the property conditions of stores, clean and green the corridors, organize shop owners and market corridors should be boosted to $4 million per year with a mix of local and federal funds. The City should allocate at least $1 million in local funds to leverage another $1 million from the state through the ReCLAIM program to finance mixed-use developments on our neighborhood corridors that could help small businesses and residents alike. The Philadelphia CDC Tax Credit Program, which supports neighborhood economic development, should be expanded.

The Kenney Administration should continue and improve efforts to increase hiring of Minority, Women and Disabled Owned Business Enterprises (M/W/DBEs) and workers in projects where public funds are involved by maintaining a commitment to Equal Opportunity Plans (EOPs), and should monitor closely how the expansion of EOPs to include goals for hiring of city residents is being implemented. The Mayor should also use his leadership to gain a commitment from developers and their contractors to create EOPs and reports for large projects that are not publicly subsidized. Large employers in Philadelphia have an important role to play in advancing Equitable Development, and the Mayor should do more to bring them to the table by encouraging them to source more of their services locally, as well as prioritize hiring from the local workforce.

4. Understand the Threats and Impacts of Displacement and Expand Assistance Programs

One of the greatest fears about gentrification is involuntary displacement: long-time residents and small businesses that want to stay in their neighborhoods but can no longer afford rising rents or property taxes. There is much we don't know about displacement: how many people does it affect and what happens to them if they are displaced? Policy makers need to collect better data to understand what's happening in our neighborhoods and craft effective policy solutions, particularly for small businesses and residential renters for whom few protections exist. The existing measures to protect homeowners from displacement due to rising property taxes must be better promoted, and homeowners must be educated about the value of their growing asset and how to manage it in their own best interest. More can be done to help small business and residential renters to provide them with stability in improving communities, and give them more notice when rents are increasing.

5. Attack Blight, Vacancy, and Abandonment in All Neighborhoods

Decades of disinvestment in some of our neighborhoods and declining conditions in once-stable neighborhoods have created a scourge of vacant lots, abandoned buildings, and poor property conditions, harming those that chose to remain, or who can't afford to live in more attractive, safer neighborhoods. These blighted conditions further strip wealth from neighborhood property owners, as home values near vacant properties are decreased by an average of $8,000 according to a recent study.[3] The City took major steps by making the Philadelphia Land Bank operational in

2015 in order to more strategically address vacant properties and get them into productive re-use more quickly, as well as improved Code enforcement on vacant properties in order to hold owners accountable to their neighbors. City Council and the Kenney Administration must maintain a strong commitment to both of these strategies, ensure that L&I has adequate resources to hold landlords accountable for poor property conditions, and help low-income homeowners become Code compliant through assistance with needed repairs.

This platform is not the answer to all of Philadelphia's problems. Economic inequality, low wages, high poverty, high crime rates, etc., are a complex set of problems that need to be attacked at many angles. But as a network of community development corporations, this is our field's contribution to that important work.

Since we published our platform in February 2015, progress has been made on many of these recommendations under the leadership of former Mayor Nutter, Mayor Kenney, Council President Clarke and several other City Council members. We have significant momentum at the start of 2016 to protect long-time residents and small businesses from being displaced, and encourage new development, residents and investments. We can do both, and we must, because it's not an option to ignore the deep inequalities in income and opportunity that hold so many Philadelphians back. It holds our entire city and region back as well. Equitable Development is a pro-growth strategy focused on attacking that inequality.

Notes

1. "Gentrification and Residential Mobility in Philadelphia," Lei Ding and Eileen Divringi, Federal Reserve Bank of Philadelphia; and Jackelyn Hwang, Princeton University. December 2015.

2. "Where Is the Land of Opportunity?" Chetty, Hendren, Kline, Saez and Turner, The Equality of Opportunity Project at Harvard University. June 2014.

3. Vacant Land Management in Philadelphia: the Costs of the Current System and the Benefits of Reform (Executive Summary). By Econsult Solutions for PACDC and the Philadelphia Redevelopment Authority, 2010. Available at: http://www.phillylandbank .org/reports#sthash.YVMplpeV.dpuf

"*In the process of constant attack,
gentrification has been accused of a
wide array of crimes.*"

There Are Solutions to the Economic Imbalances of Gentrification

Daniel Fernández

In the following viewpoint, Daniel Fernández discusses gentrification as a term that receives endless bad press for its supposed effect on low-income neighborhood residents. The author argues that gentrification is about the value of land, how the land is used, and the productivity of residents and that these factors are what drive economics and gentrification. Fernández is the founder of UFM Market Trends and a professor of economics at the Francisco Marroquín University.

As you read, consider the following questions:

1. Is gentrification a "new monster to be fought"? Why or why not?
2. How do the statistics cited support the author's argument?
3. How does the productivity of residents relate to housing prices in their area?

"Gentrification—and Tourism—Have Become the New Target in the Never-Ending Social Struggle in Favor of the Disadvantaged," by Daniel Fernández, Universidad Francisco Marroquín, October 16, 2017. Reprinted by permission. This article was originally published by UFM Market Trends (trends.ufm.edu/en).

G entrification is the new monster to be fought. The term already has such a bad press, that almost no one is willing to say anything in its favor—defending gentrification and defending neoliberalism are now almost interchangeable.

In the process of constant attack, gentrification has been accused of a wide array of crimes: destroying local commerce by promoting "economic monoculture," the incomprehensible "reduction of walkability," and being accused of promoting infidelity—from neighborhoods to its residents. The enemies of free and voluntary trade, which always lack arguments, do not spare adjectives to discredit the term—which almost always comes in the vague form of "economic interests."

What Is Gentrification?

The definitions are not always innocent. Gentrifications comes from the word *Gentry*. Its meaning is associated with nobility or people of high birth—it also refers to the bourgeoisie.

Gentrification would be the process by which the original residents of a sector or neighborhood—generally centric and popular—are progressively displaced by others with higher purchasing power.

Who could be in favor of gentrification? Isn't it just another battle in the endless war between the upper classes and the disadvantaged? To shed light on this matter, let's examine what the value of housing depends on.

What Do Housing Prices Depend On? On the Productivity of Its Inhabitants

Housing—like any other capital asset—derives its value from the many uses that can be done with it. To greater and more valued uses, the higher the price of the house. When a house loses its ability to provide housing services, it loses a great deal of its value— or all.

The most common use for housing is to provide rooming services for the resident of a city. When the inhabitants of a city are very productive, housing is generally more expensive than in places where inhabitants are less productive. Greater wealth leads to a greater capacity to push housing prices up. More high-paid people lead to higher housing prices.

This is why larger and richer cities are the cities where most of the housing price is attributed to land values—an element that is necessarily part of every housing unit and by which only constructing taller buildings can the shortage be temporarily stalled.

This explains how cities that have little geographical space, are cities that usually have the most skyscrapers. It also explains why housing prices are so high in cities that have very tight restrictions to build skyscrapers, such as London.

In the United States we can see how the most powerful places are also those that have higher housing prices and where the price of land is a larger part of the total price of the unit.

	AVERAGE HOUSEHOLD VALUE ($)	LAND AS A % OF HOUSING VALUE
Midwest	192.000	36%
Southeast	187.000	42%
Southwest	179.000	38%
East Coast	376.000	64%
West Coast	568.000	74%

Source: Davis & Palumbo (2006). Data from 2004.

Land that is in areas with large populations is much more valued than land in areas with small populations—relative soil scarcity and greater wealth are the most important elements. With the data from the United States, we can see how this is true.

POPULATION	AVERAGE PRICE PER ACRE ($)
Between 10.000 y 50.000 inhabitants (not adjacent to a big city)	3.473
Between 10.000 y 50.000 inhabitants (adjacent to a big city)	6.681
Less than 1 million inhabitants	16.558
More than 1 million inhabitants	64.844

Source: Larson (2015). Data from 2009.

Alternate Uses

Providing rooms to city dwellers is not the only use that can be given to a housing unit or building. With the help of new investment—complementary capital—the housing can be remodeled to serve as business office or to provide rooming services for tourists.

Not all housing units can be adapted to these alternative uses. Not every building can be easily converted into office space. The location factor of an office is important for the establishment of an office in a place that was not initially designed for that purpose (for example, the construction would be far away from a cluster of companies).

Similarly, not all housing units can be adapted to provide services to tourists. The location of the real estate is essentially important. Units that are hard to access or are far away from tourist areas will have little demand for overnight stays, and therefore their alternative use for tourism will not even be taken into account.

The uses of housing, although limited, do not end there. The following are illustrative examples that in no way exhaust the possible uses of real estate imagined by entrepreneurs.

The Economic Meaning of Gentrification

Let's see what happens to the inhabitants of a city—or a zone of a city—when the number of possible uses for individual dwellings increases. To this end, we will differentiate between homeowners and tenants.

Homeowners

People who own their homes—or land and other constructions—see the prices of their houses increase. As previously mentioned, the greater the amount of possible competition for uses of homes, the greater push of those that want to make use of those housing units.

A higher price of housing increases the wealth of the homeowners of those particular units.

If the neighbors decide to continue living in the same property, they do so at a higher opportunity cost. If they were to lease or sell their property, they could make a large profit just because they were lucky enough to be in the right place, at the right time.

Tenants

By increasing the number of uses and their value, the price of housing tends to skyrocket. Those who usually complain most about gentrification are tenants who rent apartments.

They claim that they are the ones being "evicted" from the homes they do not own—not the owners—because they can't pay a higher rent.

This is true. However, there is a question that analysis on gentrification usually does not address: Are there any benefits for the tenants?

The Advantages for Traditional Tenants

Traditional tenants seem to be the main losers when it comes to gentrification. However, gentrification does have benefits to these tenants through other means.

New uses given housing units provide services to businesses or tourists only through the help of complementary factors, including work. The new economic activity that is competing for the uses of housing also competes for the labor of the city's residents.

This means that the economic activities that require the rental of housing units need workers—and other productive factors—to be able to develop.

The new economic activities that are developed push up the price of rent. However, they also increase wages in the labor market—or reduce unemployment if it exists.

This means that the same process that makes residential housing more scarce also makes work scarce. This explains why the wealthiest cities are also the cities where rents tend to be higher.

Analyzing gentrification by looking at its alleged costs in the form of higher rental prices for housing is the same as only looking at one side of a coin. Prohibiting tourism or other alternative uses for housing only generates a fall in incomes complementary to those uses—such as labor—ultimately leading to the expulsion of viable and sustainable businesses and the discouragement of profitable economic sectors.

Fighting gentrification is synonymous with low wages, unemployment, and poverty.

High Wages and Low Rents?

It would seem that we have two mutually exclusive options: cities with higher wages and higher housing prices, or cities with lower wages and lower housing prices. In terms of purchasing power parity, both options are equally desirable—or undesirable. Then, are we limited between only these two options? Not really.

If the aim is to combat high rent prices, rather than prohibit economic activities—which lower economic growth and wages—it would be much easier to cover the greater demand for housing services with greater supply—more housing units.

It seems that the proposed solution for gentrification always involves restricting the demand of those obscure "economic interests." However, this option is clearly inferior to the alternative of allowing an increase in real estate supply by lifting restrictions on construction.

The price per square meter in London is more than double that of New York's, yet New York has a 45% higher salary than Britain's capital.

	PRICE PER SQUARE METER ($)	AVERAGE WAGES ($)
London	34.531	47.510
New York	17.191	68.708

Source: Global Property Guide. Payscale

The difference between the two cities lies in the fact that, although both have draconian laws towards new construction, London is much stricter than New York when it comes to building skyscrapers. Regulation makes land values artificially expensive.

A deregulation in the real estate market can certainly help lower the rent prices and houses without having to restrict access to businesses and economic sectors that can bring prosperity in the areas where they are established.

VIEWPOINT

> *"In a deindustrialized small city like
> North Adams, Massachusetts, for
> example, gentrification is welcomed."*

Gentrification Can Save Smaller Cities
Jonathan Wynn and Andrew Deener

In the following viewpoint, Jonathan Wynn and Andrew Deener argue that, while gentrification is considered a dirty word in large cities like New York and Los Angeles, there is evidence to show that it can have overwhelmingly positive effects in small cities such as Austin and Nashville. The authors contend that there are different kinds of gentrification and that some of the country's cities need it. Wynn is an associate professor of sociology at the University of Massachusetts–Amherst. Deener is an associate professor of sociology at the University of Connecticut.

As you read, consider the following questions:

1. Why are storefronts on New York City's Bleecker Street empty?
2. What institution has transformed the former industrialized city of North Adams, Massachusetts?
3. What city hired the nation's first chief storyteller?

I n July, a group of long-time, mostly Latino residents of Los Angeles's Boyle Heights neighborhood staged protests outside a trendy new coffee shop called Weird Wave Coffee, holding signs that read "Amerikkkano" and "WHITE COFFEE."

Across the country in Brooklyn's rapidly gentrifying Crown Heights neighborhood, locals lashed out over a new restaurant with decor that included fake bullet holes and a menu that offered a drink called "40 ounce rosé" (malt liquor and wine) served in a paper bag.

Over the past few decades, gentrification debates have migrated from the pages of academic journals into the streets and the mainstream press.

The word, in many ways, is tinged with negativity. And for good reason. In tight real estate markets, it can lead to development that privileges profits over community and shuts people out of neighborhoods they have lived in for decades.

But what about cities struggling to overcome the threat of bankruptcy like Hartford? How does gentrification look in New South cities like Austin and Nashville, where midcentury urban planning destroyed residential communities and left downtowns largely unoccupied?

While doing research on the economic health of Hartford, one of us asked the head of a downtown Hartford nonprofit about gentrification. Her response? "We could use some of that. But we are so far away from it, it's not even an issue."

If residential patterns and urban areas vary, so too must the story of gentrification. In other words: Have big cities hijacked the gentrification debate?

The Origins of Gentrification

"Gentrification" is a term coined by the British sociologist Ruth Glass in 1964 to explain the return of the middle class to London's center city.

In the US, academics and urban planners first started extensively talking about and debating gentrification in the 1970s. Between

1950 and 1970, urban manufacturing went overseas and white middle-class city-dwellers moved to the suburbs. Concerns over blighted urban centers grew. Sociologists, planners and geographers found new cultural and economic trends to study related to the rise of artist and middle-class loft living and the return of capital investment to urban centers.

Today, the meaning of gentrification no longer refers to the "return to the center." Instead, it usually means that new and affluent residents or developers are investing in a neighborhood.

This infusion of capital changes the relationships within and between communities. Demand increases and property values rise; poorer residents are displaced as wealthier people move in; new shops appear and the public image of the neighborhood changes. High demand can incentivize landlords to evict residents, at times using egregious practices—like hiring someone to harass renters— in order to escalate rental prices.

Extreme gentrification takes place in the highest-rent, highest-demand places like San Francisco or New York's Greenwich Village. Rents in New York's once-booming Bleecker Street have become so astronomical that vacancy is now a problem of too much demand, rather than not enough: Property owners now keep their storefronts empty, hoping a major chain will want to locate in the high-visibility district.

Gentrification isn't all negative. In an influential and counterintuitive study, Lance Freeman and Frank Braconi, who study urban development, found that poorer residents were less likely to move out of gentrifying neighborhoods than nongentrifying neighborhoods. Safety improves with gentrification, and so can services and amenities.

While some neighborhoods experience positive outcomes, gentrification studies are mostly concerned with access to housing, public space and the loss of community. It seems impossible not to view New York, San Francisco, Los Angeles or Boston through the lens of skyrocketing real estate and displaced residents.

What about other kinds of places?

The Urban In-Between

When cities experienced population and economic decline decades ago, some, like New York and Boston, found ways to rebound. Others, like Detroit or Connecticut's capital city, Hartford, did not.

Hartford continues to experience unusual and difficult financial circumstances. The city has low home-ownership rates and high poverty rates. But maybe more significant is that the city is the state's capital. Half of the city's real estate is made up of government buildings, educational facilities or hospitals—all of which are nontaxable. With a US$65 million deficit, Hartford is now on the verge of bankruptcy.

Where is Hartford's gentrification? Or, more precisely, is there a kind of gentrification that would be welcomed in a city like Hartford? A place like Hartford could learn from smaller cities, which are less afflicted by the bloated real estate and speculation that plague places like New York and San Francisco.

In a deindustrialized small city like North Adams, Massachusetts, for example, gentrification is welcomed. The old mill city near the Berkshire Mountains had its sprawling electrical manufacturing plant, Sprague Electric, transformed into a contemporary fine art museum, MASS MoCA. The museum, in turn, helped transform the city from a shrinking post-industrial community into an arts and cultural destination. The museum injected $34.4 million into the local economy in 2015, drawing tourists, lowering unemployment levels and creating opportunities for new businesses.

Tourism jobs are not the skilled union jobs Sprague Electric once offered. But without other opportunities, the community welcomes this kind of gentrification. The town was built for 20,000, but only has 13,000 residents. The community wants—indeed, it needs—more people.

There is also what we could call "empty lot" gentrification. Gentrification doesn't always displace existing populations. Consider cities like Nashville, Tennessee and Austin, Texas, where suburbs bloomed in the postwar era. The center cities never housed the heavy manufacturing of northeastern and Rust Belt cities; until recently, they remained sites of light manufacturing, parking garages and empty lots.

In the early 2000s, former Austin mayor (and real estate entrepreneur) Will Wynn sought to build more residential properties in downtown Austin, and Austin has since seen dramatic residential growth. Empty lot gentrification has its own issues: It can create downtowns for elites. Concerns over gentrification beyond Austin's city center have grown, and Austin's famed music venues are getting priced out.

A Tale of Two Kinds of Cities

In bloated real estate markets like New York or San Francisco, critics of gentrification see even the smallest changes—a new park or a new coffee shop—as harbingers for inevitable neighborhood ruin.

For cities needing gentrification, the issues are different. The conversation about popular cities has made academics and policy analysts timid about gentrification. Ailing small cities need to increase visibility to attract more people and develop a stable tax-base.

Hardly a call for free market-driven housing policy, there is no reason policies that minimize the negative effects of gentrification—rent control, mixed income housing and limited equity cooperatives—cannot be combined with efforts to attract the middle class.

The gentrification debates should also not blind us to what made New York and San Francisco attractive cities in the first place. The principles of urban activist Jane Jacobs for healthy city life still hold: diverse uses of streets and public places, mixed-use buildings, a variety of economic and commercial opportunities and local excitement about community building.

But simply getting people into the city cannot be overlooked. In North Adams, new opportunities come from investing in the arts. In Pittsburgh, an openness to technical innovation, museums, universities and a dynamic restaurant culture are creating national buzz about a city that continues to lose population. Detroit just hired the nation's first chief story-teller to help move the narrative away from stale stereotypes. Throughout European cities, night mayors are charged with inspiring excitement around urban nightlife.

Hartford will never become New York. But why not look to North Adams, Pittsburgh or Columbus for examples of a different kind of gentrification?

Weird Wave Coffee, in other words, might be welcomed in Connecticut.

> "While a modest number of homeowners
> have benefited from the changes,
> renters ... are likely to be displaced
> from their neighborhood just as the
> schools and services are improving."

Enforce Stricter Regulations to Stop Greedy Landlords

Brad Lander

Advocates of redevelopment and the resulting gentrification claim that the process creates more diverse neighborhoods, but in the following viewpoint, Brad Lander states that it does not actually reduce segregation in cities. The author argues that gentrification is an issue about equal opportunity and equal choices for everyone, not just for those with higher incomes. Lander is a New York City Council member representing Brooklyn's 39th District and the council's deputy leader for policy.

As you read, consider the following questions:

1. Why has redevelopment failed in preserving diversity?
2. What are some of the author's suggestions for making the city less segregated?
3. How do the author's experiences and credentials, mentioned in the article, support his opinion in the article?

"It'll Take More than a Voucher," by Brad Lander, Furman Center for Real Estate and Urban Policy, May 2014. Reprinted by permission.

As Rachel Godsil writes, it is intellectually tempting—but currently misguided—to think of gentrification as a solution to the segregation that divides New York City.

I've been grappling uneasily with this tension for the past 20 years, at the Fifth Avenue Committee (whose founding mission in 1977 was to confront displacement and preserve diversity in Park Slope), the Pratt Center for Community Development, as a past board chair of ANHD, and for the past five years representing much of "Brownstone Brooklyn" in the New York City Council.

We've built and preserved hundreds of units of affordable housing, helped thousands of people find good jobs in growing sectors, pioneered new "inclusionary zoning" and 421-a tax incentive policies, and helped to preserve rent regulations.

But we certainly have not succeeded in preserving diversity. Rents and home prices are no longer affordable for young professionals, much less teachers or artists, much less old-timers or low-income families. Even in those places where there's a bit more diversity within a few blocks (e.g. near subsidized housing), the schools often remain more segregated than the neighborhood.

Don't get me wrong. I love my community—its great public schools, parks, livable streets, and locally-owned businesses—and yes, its contradictory but very real commitment to social justice and fighting inequality. We remain keenly aware of the contradictions (and not only because we're all reading Thomas Piketty this month).

Even as gentrification and immigration have taken a bit off its rough edges, NYC remains firmly segregated. We've seen the smallest declines in segregation of any big city in the US and we're second-highest in racial segregation. Economic segregation is growing, with fewer mixed-income neighborhoods, and more very wealthy and very poor ones.

New York's schools are the most racially segregated in the country. And as Aaron Pallas writes, this is true even in gentrifying neighborhoods like Park Slope, where the (zone-based) neighborhood schools re-segregate rapidly and dramatically.

GENTRIFICATION AND CREDIT SCORES

Gentrification hasn't forced out as many residents as one might think, according to a new study by the Federal Reserve Bank of Philadelphia. Rather, after assessing financial health in residents from 2002 to 2014, researchers found that the number of people moving from gentrifying neighborhoods into pricier, higher-income areas was higher than those who moved due to economic pressures.

Still, their findings didn't leave much to celebrate. When homing in on financially disadvantaged movers, research revealed that these residents often moved to worse-off areas with poorer quality-of-life indicators.

"We found fairly compelling evidence that a lot of demographic change in gentrifying neighborhoods was driven more by the changes in who was able to move into those neighborhoods," researcher Eileen Divringi says. "Ours is the first study that's really been able to track where individuals are moving. A lot of prior studies had found that financially vulnerable residents weren't necessarily more likely to move … [but] the picture was somewhat limited there."

The authors found that Philadelphians with mortgages weren't more keen to move. In many cases, low-score movers in the River Wards relocated to neighborhoods similar to ones they were leaving.

While a modest number of homeowners have benefited from the changes, renters (outside of subsidized housing) are likely to be displaced from their neighborhood just as the schools and services are improving. New Yorkers are mostly renters. Lower-income New Yorkers are overwhelmingly renters.

Godsil is also right that gentrification compels government action in order to make sure more residents benefit. While the more highly-linked articles about gentrification are cultural (not that "Dream Revisited" won't give Spike Lee, Errol Louis, and A.O. Scott a run for their money), for me the policy issues are ones of class and opportunity. Our goal should not be to engineer neighborhood culture. But it should be to offer far more equality in life chances.

Compare this to the gentrification seen in Center City and West Philadelphia, areas with fewer homeowners, where low-score movers tended to end up in areas with higher unemployment, lower home values and poorer quality of life.

West Philadelphia holds some the of the most sought-after neighborhoods in the city, but not everyone was downgrading. Movers in this section left for more favorable settings overall, researchers found. The poor outcomes were limited here to the economically vulnerable.

The researchers noted that neighbors who stayed put saw their credit scores improve, the highest jump recorded in areas with the most gentrification (an average 23 points over the course of three years). Among those who moved though, results were "uneven."

A common gentrification question has been: But where are the displaced moving to? High-score movers often went to places that were easy to predict, like University City (where Penn and Drexel are) and the suburbs. Low-score movers were dispersed throughout the city, more likely to reach neighborhoods farther out from the core. Low-score renters who moved often went to areas with higher crime, worse schools, and … fewer jobs and higher unemployment rates.

"How Gentrification Can Affect Your Credit Score," by Cassie Owens, Next City, October 23, 2015.

But confronting the problem of gentrification—with a commitment to real equality of opportunity—is far harder than Godsil acknowledges with her prescription for "gentrification vouchers."

For starters, it's too expensive—and even self-defeating—to offer subsidies that would affirm and fuel the speculative increases in land prices that are driving displacement.

A bizarre but horrible case in point, right now, is the mass-eviction of over 100 seniors (in their 80s, 90s, and 100s, including a Holocaust survivor and a Tuskegee airman) from the Prospect Park Residence. These residents pay over $5,000 per month (admittedly, for a meal plan and some services, in addition to rent). But they are being cruelly evicted by a landlord whose base greed simply knows no limits. He's making plenty, but now that the J-51 tax abatement has expired, and he can take the building to market-rate, he can make far more.

Gentrification vouchers for the seniors at the Prospect Park Residence would cost far more than we could justify subsidizing—and they still wouldn't abate the trauma of a 102-year-old great-grandmother, forced to move many miles away and see her great-grandkids far less often.

Of course we want to leverage the benefits of growth in a more equal way. But if we actually want "neighborhoods of choice and opportunity," we have to be willing to do more to temper, regulate, and redistribute the speculative increases themselves. Toward that end, I believe we should embrace stronger regulatory tools that might give values of decency and equality a fighting chance:

- Strengthen the rent laws. Let's start (next year in Albany) by rolling back vacancy decontrol (without which those seniors might not be facing the heave-ho) and demanding local control over our own rent laws. Operating multifamily rental property in NYC is good business. We don't need to allow super-profits to owners looking to convert their buildings, out of some sense of obligation to the market. I'm pleased to see that Rachel Godsil has just been named chair of NYC's Rent Guidelines Board, where she'll have a hand in shaping NYC's rent regulation policy. In gentrifying places outside of New York, policy-makers might want to consider the intriguing contemporary model of selective rent regulation proposed by Arlo Chase.

- Mandatory inclusionary zoning, to insist on affordable units in all new developments (and get more where we are willing to give density bonuses and tax breaks). Hopefully new requirements would moderate spiraling land prices a little bit, as the affordability obligation gets built into the price of land.

- Permanent affordability of subsidized housing, to better prevent families from being pushed out at the end of the regulatory period. We've seen too many cases now where families were evicted and affordability lost, for a return that developers never imagined or relied on when they negotiated the deal 30 years earlier.

- More durable mixed-use: Its not only residents that get pushed out, but businesses too. We've got a real opportunity in Gowanus to preserve blue-collar jobs, some room for arts and industry, and a mixed-use neighborhood—even as we permit some new residential development. But only if we include far stronger zoning tools to protect manufacturing and mixed-use areas (and provide for the infrastructure needed to sustain smart growth)—as we're aiming to do through our "Bridging Gowanus" community planning effort.

- Perhaps most important, confront school segregation head-on. We're experimenting in Park Slope, with a new model we adopted last year at PS 133 (a new, non-zoned school, with admissions criteria that prioritize diversity), and other districts across the city are doing even more. As growth leads to building new schools, rather than provide them with a segregated geographic zone, we should adopt admissions policies that prioritize diversity. More broadly, we should make a real, citywide plan to reduce school segregation.

I'm not naïve. We aren't going to hold back market-forces. I'm willing to support smart growth and development, even where some of my constituents resist it. And even as I'm nostalgic, I like a lot of what's new—even the new "shuffleboard club" in Gowanus (ok, not quite as much as the old slot-car racing track in Kensington)— much of which has been driven by the "creative destruction" of market-led gentrification. I'm not aiming for some ideal society. And I'm mindful of the messy consequences of regulation.

But it's not the market that has delivered us Prospect Park, or my kids' public schools, or a livable and walkable neighborhood, or our neighborhood libraries, or the affordable housing units that remain.

And it won't be the market—even tempered with some vouchers—that confronts the crisis of inequality and allows our neighborhoods to be shared a little better.

If I missed something, and Congress is preparing to address steadily-growing inequality more fundamentally with new macroeconomic policies, I'm willing to give those a chance to work first. But last I noticed, the Democratic-majority Senate couldn't pass a bill raising the minimum wage to a paltry $10.10 (which would net a full-time worker an $18,400 annual salary, enough to affordably pay a whopping $460 in rent per month).

So I'm ready for some bolder policies at the local level—stronger than Godsil recommends, ones that I know my friends at REBNY and the Partnership for NYC will roll their eyes at—to see if we can build on the successes we have, and make it possible for a far-wider set of New Yorkers to share them.

"Gentrifying neighborhoods
on average do not experience
consistent, meaningful gains in
local employment."

Gentrification of Low-Income Neighborhoods Does Not Result in Gains to Local Employment

Rachel Meltzer and Pooya Ghorbani

One of the common arguments against gentrification is that it displaces neighborhood residents to accommodate newer, more economically privileged people. However, existing research has not produced any conclusive evidence that incumbent residents are systematically displaced under circumstances of gentrification. In the following excerpted viewpoint, Rachel Meltzer and Pooya Ghorbani explore whether or not the residents that appear to stay in gentrifying neighborhoods benefit from the economic and social changes. The authors find that residents actually have fewer job opportunities in the immediate neighborhood but larger gains in employment opportunities farther away from their home neighborhood. Meltzer is Assistant Professor of Urban Policy and Chair of the Public and Urban Policy Program at the New School in New York City. Ghorbani is a PhD candidate in public and urban policy at the New School.

"Does Gentrification Increase Employment Opportunities in Low-Income Neighborhoods?" by Rachel Meltzer and Pooya Ghorbani, June 15, 2017. Reprinted by permission.

As you read, consider the following questions:

1. What does the article conclude about employment opportunities in gentrifying neighborhoods?
2. What kinds of new jobs do go to current neighborhood residents?
3. What specific reasons do the authors cite for their argument about employment opportunities in these neighborhoods?

G entrification is a term often associated with displacement and other negative byproducts of affluent in-movers altering the economic and demographic composition of a neighborhood. Empirical research on neighborhood change, however, has not produced any conclusive evidence that incumbent residents are systematically displaced under circumstances of gentrification. This raises the question, do these incumbent residents benefit from the economic and social changes that accompany gentrification? In this paper, we focus on low-income neighborhoods undergoing economic transitions (i.e. gentrification) and test whether or not the potential benefits from these changes stay within the community, in the form of employment opportunities for local residents. We find that employment effects from gentrification are quite localized. Incumbent residents experience meaningful job losses within their home census tract, even while jobs overall increase. In our preferred model, local jobs decline by as much as 63 percent. These job losses are concentrated in service and goods-producing sectors and low- and moderate-wage positions. Proximate job losses, however, are compensated for by larger gains in goods-producing and low-wage jobs slightly farther away. There is some evidence that chain establishments are associated with modest job gains in gentrifying census tracts, and that, outside of NYC, businesses that stay in place around gentrifying neighborhoods are associated with marginal job gains.

[…]

Theoretical Motivation

While the entry of new money and investment into a community can "price out" incumbent, typically lower-income residents, this increased economic activity can also bring new opportunities for local residents. One potential upside to gentrification is more nearby employment opportunities; the extent of this benefit will depend on whether or not and to what degree these new jobs actually go to local residents. However, the impact of neighborhood economic upgrading on employment opportunities for local residents is theoretically ambiguous.

Economic upgrading not only brings in more affluent and educated residents, but it also ushers in services that did not previously pervade those markets (Meltzer and Schuetz, 2012; Meltzer and Capperis, 2014). Both of these additions to the community can facilitate access to localized employment opportunities. First, it is possible that the residential integration of relatively more affluent and educated households could impose both direct and indirect positive externalities on incumbent residents, who also tend to be lower-income and less educated. Indirect effects, akin to peer effects, would come simply out of exposure to this new population, whether or not any direct interaction took place (Ellen and Turner, 1997; Galster, 2012). More likely is the employment opportunities that come out of direct contact with new, perhaps more networked or more enterprising neighbors (Ioannides and Loury, 2004). Both would result in a positive impact on access to employment opportunities, the direct more significantly than the indirect. Whether or not employment opportunities are local remains ambiguous, unless the new neighbor is also more likely to personally hire in his or her home or local business.

A perhaps more convincing scenario is where economic change brings in new and/or more local business establishments, i.e. those entities that actually hire. First, the likelihood to hire locally will depend on the type of business. More service-oriented businesses, or those that do not require technical or more advanced skill training, will more likely be able to hire from a local pool that may not have higher or more technical levels of educational attainment (Hellerstein et al., 2015). Second, the search costs for both the businesses and local residents are lower: information about the employment opportunities is accessible and transparent (i.e. local residents can see when a new business is opening up) and advertising for available positions can penetrate the local community immediately (Johnson, 2006). Finally, government policies may require local hiring for new businesses, especially those in brand new developments or renovations (that are also more likely to receive public subsidies or permitting). All else equal, these mechanisms predict increased local employment opportunities— essentially a reversal of the spatial mismatch phenomenon.

On the other hand, physical integration may not translate into economic integration. Should neighborhood economic upgrading bring in new businesses that more productively use the existing commercial space (i.e. hire those with more technical training) or who exploit farther-reaching hiring networks (chain establishments, for example), local existing residents, with potentially lower skill sets and smaller networks, will not be as competitively positioned for these jobs. In addition, local businesses may simply discriminate against potential local hires, based on race or class, which would lower the chances of local employment (Lang and Lehmann, 2012).

[…]

Localized Economic Opportunity and Gentrification

Even though the empirical evidence indicates that incumbent residents tend to stay in their gentrifying neighborhoods, we know very little about how they experience the potential opportunities that accompany neighborhood change. Do existing residents benefit from local gains in services and employment opportunities? A handful of studies focus on changes in commercial services (i.e. retail), in neighborhoods undergoing economic and demographic transitions. The economically upgrading neighborhoods tend to experience higher growth rates in local retail establishments and employment (Meltzer and Schuetz, 2012; Schuetz et al., 2012). In their case-study analysis of gentrifying neighborhoods in New York City, Zukin et al. (2009) also observe retail growth, but more so for independently owned establishments compared to chain ones. Immergluck (1999) finds that neighborhoods that are relatively more minority and less affluent experience declines in commercial investment, as measured by changes in permit activity. Chapple and Jacobus (2009) observe retail revitalization most significantly in middle-income neighborhoods that are economically upgrading. Therefore, the literature implies that gentrifying neighborhoods do tend to witness an increase in commercial activity, likely due to the changing consumer population and the (perceived) increase in demand for goods and services in areas that were not previously seen as viable investments (Carree and Thurik, 1996).

Other studies have taken a different perspective, focusing instead on the production side. Curran (2004) conducts a case-study analysis in the Williamsburg neighborhood of Brooklyn, a historically manufacturing and blue-collar neighborhood that has, in recent years, undergone extensive gentrification. She finds evidence of gentrification-induced industrial displacement that has degraded local blue-collar work and forced much of it into the informal sector. Lester and Hartley (2014) also observe industrial restructuring in gentrifying neighborhoods, such that jobs in restaurants and retail services tend to replace those in goods producing industries. Furthermore, gentrifying neighborhoods experienced both more rapid employment growth and more rapid industrial restructuring than other, non-gentrifying neighborhoods. While Lester and Hartley conclude that gentrification is itself a catalyst for localized industrial restructuring, Kolko (2009) raises the important point that gentrification is also induced (and perpetuated) by the influx of affluent households who are presumably following higher paying jobs. In his study, Kolko focuses on neighborhoods located in or near the central business district and estimates the impact of changes in job pay on the

If You Can Weather the Changes

Many Philadelphia neighborhoods are rapidly changing, leaving some wondering if the current wave of gentrification is a blessing or a curse for low-income residents.

The answer is complicated, but a new analysis from the Federal Reserve Bank of Philadelphia finds one thing is clear: if vulnerable residents are able to weather the changes, they're poised for better lives.

Higher-income people moving in does indeed mean positive changes—improving public schools, ebbing violent crime, creating locally owned businesses.

The flip side, though, is that when housing costs shoot up too quickly, vulnerable residents are pushed out and often end up in poorer neighborhoods.

Then there are the people who seemingly get caught in the middle.

"For individuals who could absorb those housing-cost increases, they might be more motivated to stay in those neighborhoods because they see neighborhood conditions improving," she said.

The report found that if people can ride out the gentrification, even if they are just scraping by, the results can be very good.

"Now that is because there is a multiplier effect happening," said Villanova University economist David Fiorenza, who has served as a consultant for cities on mitigating the negative effects of gentrification.

average neighborhood income (his proxy for gentrification). Baum-Snow and Hartley (2017) conduct a slightly augmented analysis, in the same vein, that comes to similar conclusions: the demand for living in certain neighborhoods due to nearby job opportunities, especially those closer to the central business district, can influence the economic trajectory of those neighborhoods. These analyses shed light on the influence of "newcomers" on local labor markets and how they too might be competing for neighborhood-based employment opportunities. No study to date tests whether or not these employment benefits are realized by incumbent residents, or how access to employment might vary by job type or broader

"So if you renew an area—and you renew it with jobs that have been created that are better than the jobs that were there before— then that means wages are up, benefits are up," he said.

Angel Rodriguez, who works with the Latino-based economic development organization Asociación Puertorriqueños en Marcha, said change is inevitable and growth is a good thing, but quality of life needs to be maintained for everyone.

"Do they want a safe environment? Yes. Do they want quality housing? Yes. Do they want great schools? Yes. Do I wanna eat, you know, fairly priced nutrient-rich food? Yes.

"And I don't think you'll find anyone who says they don't want that," he said.

What tips the balance in deciding whether a family can stay, or is forced to leave, often comes down to chance, Rodriguez said. A health emergency. A cut in hours. A layoff. All those things can make or break a family sorting through the ramifications of gentrification.

"It is rent. It's food prices, depending on family size, can you actually feed your family?" he said.

**"Gentrification Can Benefit Poorer Residents as Well as Wealthier Neighbors,"
Bobby Allyn, WHYY.org, December 16, 2015.**

neighborhood conditions. This link is crucial, as it more directly measures how the benefits of gentrification are retained by local community members, or if they are exported to those without any longstanding community ties.

[...]

Conclusion

Since the dark days of the 1970s and 1980s, many urban cores have experienced dramatic comebacks. This turn-around has brought economic prosperity to places that had not witnessed it in some time. It also has presented challenges to those who could not afford to sustain the rising rents and costs of living that tend to accompany gentrification. The empirical research on gentrification, however, has not supported the displacement hypothesis and in fact shows that a number of residents stay and benefit from the improved quality of life. With gentrification comes increased investment and economic activity more generally, and in this paper we test whether or not local residents, in low-income neighborhoods undergoing economic upgrading, benefit from nearby employment opportunities.

We find that employment effects from gentrification are quite localized. Incumbent residents experience meaningful job losses within their home census tract, even while jobs overall increase. These results are robust to models stratifying the sample based on the concentration of incumbents and using Bartik income shocks to instrument for actual income growth. Specifically, local jobs decline by as much as 63 percent (about 19 off of a base of 30 in the typical census tract). These job losses are concentrated in service and goods-producing sectors and low- and moderate-wage positions; but local residents do see gains in higher-wage jobs in very proximate live-work zones and lower-wage jobs slightly farther away. There is some evidence that chain establishments are associated with modest job gains in gentrifying census tracts (about 2.5 jobs on average), and that, outside of NYC, businesses that stay in place around gentrifying neighborhoods are associated with marginal job gains (i.e. less than 1 job on average).

One of the most significant take-aways from the analysis is the importance of defining the geographic span of the live-work market: any negative impact is on immediately proximate jobs (i.e. in the same tract), and job effects are more inconsistent (and often null) in larger live-work zones. Most stark, are the very localized job losses, across all types of jobs. However, these less optimistic findings are balanced by signs of benefit-enhancing changes, such as more goods-producing and higher-wage jobs within 1 mile or less of gentrifying neighborhoods. Moreover, gains in goods-producing and low-wage jobs at 1-to-2 mile distances more than compensate for the volume of localized losses. And jobs within 1-to-2 mile commuting distances, in a locality with a well- developed transit system, are arguably still very "local."

We also shed some light on the mechanisms behind the observed job changes: incumbent businesses and chain establishments may facilitate local hires and job retention. Moreover, there is meaningful variation in local job effects depending on the setting. Denser, tighter markets, like NYC, may respond differently and may therefore require different strategies in the face of gentrification.

> *"Transformation processes in Latin American cities brought the sharpening of unequal realities, dispossession, and socioeconomic segregation."*

The Government Must Strive for Balance in Urban Renewal

Maryluz Barragán

In the following viewpoint, Maryluz Barragán argues that gentrification has also affected Latin American cities, impacting the social and cultural rights of that region's economically vulnerable people and jeopardizing the culture, memory, and social capital of neighborhoods. The author contends that it is the responsibility of the state to improve urban areas while also ensuring the local identity is retained. Barragán is a lawyer who researches litigation for Dejusticia, a Colombia-based research and advocacy organization.

As you read, consider the following questions:

1. Consider how gentrification in Latin America might differ from that in the United States and Great Britain.
2. How did the UNESCO declaration of Getsemaní as a heritage site impact its gentrification?
3. What is the greatest challenge in urban planning?

"Gentrification: Borders That Amplify Inequality," by Maryluz Barragán, Dejusticia, July 24, 2017. Reprinted by permission.

Transformation processes in Latin American cities brought the sharpening of unequal realities, dispossession, and socioeconomic segregation. The restoration of old architectural structures and urban centers increases property prices, resulting in the displacement of local residents and the violation of multiple rights. This phenomenon, known as gentrification, triggers changes in the resident population, housing structures, and commercial activities, and is driven by an increase in land value due to speculative investment strategies in real estate projects. At this point, it is worth asking if it is possible to intervene in this matter given the significant impact on residents' rights, or if it is an unstoppable natural consequence of market rules in the configuration of cities.

There are serious doubts about the relevance of the term *gentrification* to explain the Latin American phenomenon since it was initially used to describe the realities of England and the United States. For Jonoschka and Sequera, although the context influences the strategies and the impact of gentrification, this global phenomenon shares consistent elements around the world given the desire of middle and upper classes to appropriate the central urban landscapes through real estate investment. Among the particularities of Latin America, these authors highlight: the role of local authorities in urban reorganization; symbolic violence involving the appropriation of cultural heritage; and material violence applied through the forced regularization of informal economies. Given the intensification of gentrification regionally, Fernando Carrión suggests that the revaluation of urban centers is due to a demographic transformation of countries: in 1950, the concentration in cities was 41%, while at the beginning of the 21st century this figure rose to 80%. Thus, the available space for urbanization is increasingly reduced.

Strong gentrification processes are evident in Colombia. A paradigmatic case is the district of Getsemaní located next to the historic center of Cartagena de Indias. After UNESCO declared the city as a world heritage site in the 1980s, private investors started buying houses in the inner city, generating rising real estate costs. In the last decade, due to the decreased supply in the area, investor interest has migrated to surrounding neighborhoods like Getsemaní. This has led to a decline in the local population of the working class neighborhood, which is also home to a great concentration of historical memory and processes during the independence period. In 2012, the neighbors conducted a population census, reporting a retention rate of native residents at 28%. In 2013, the same census showed a retention rate of 16.7%, demonstrating an alarming decline of more than 10% from one year to another. Regarding the economic conditions of the locals, 61% of these families live on the minimum wage.

The coincidence between this type of UNESCO recognition and gentrification is not exclusive to Getsemaní. This relationship is also evident in cities like Cuenca in Ecuador, Buenos Aires in Argentina and Salvador Bahia in Brazil. This is because the local authorities have prioritized maintenance and recovery of urban centers to attract foreign investment and turn these areas into attractive spaces for tourism. This has occurred without thinking about city planning in terms of the locals' enjoyment and well-being.

But gentrification experiences do not always begin with the lack of state protection for residents, which facilitates the sale of real estate and the subsequent transformation of the neighborhood. There are also processes in which the state plays a much more active role and focuses on the expulsion of informal commerce through strong policies of public space "recovery." This has occurred in Mexico, where in the mid-nineties and early 2000s the government implemented a plan for the "recovery" of the historic center in Mexico City. The plan entailed the eviction of approximately 25,000 street vendors, along with a public expenditure of more than 400 million USD, and private investment in 81 thousand square meters in houses, lodgings and offices. The resulting commercial and real estate development increased the cost of living in the area, displacing informal vendors and long-time residents.

In light of this reality, experiences of resistance developed in academic spaces and collective neighborhood actions to defend the rights of affected communities. Whereas it is not possible to advocate for the intangibility of urban centers, various groups are aiming to reduce the negative impact of urban transformations by demanding a democratization of the benefits given under the regeneration of these areas. Increasingly, the concept of the "right to the city" gains force, which is understood as the power to demand the renewal of urban spaces together with inclusion policies and thus, avoiding the indirect displacement of locals. But beyond the aspirational aspect, to what extent is there a legal "right to the city"? For Lucas Correa, this collective nature right has three dimensions: the equal enjoyment of city spaces, the possibility of collective and participatory construction in city affairs, and the effective enjoyment of human rights in urban contexts.

The right to the city is a response to the multiple challenges of city building, like gentrification, which raises a tension between past conditions of state abandonment (that are neither possible nor desirable to return to) and urban planning processes with an economic vision.

In Latin America, gentrification processes affecting social and cultural rights of economically vulnerable populations are becoming more common. In light of these scenarios, there is a clear need to accept the influence of market dynamics on the neighborhood, but also to demand the state to carry out urban transformations at the same time it protects memory, cultural expressions, and other elements that characterize our neighborhood. The challenge in urban planning is to overcome gentrification by embracing urban renewal processes that harmonize freedom and property rights with the rights of the most vulnerable, while improving their quality of life.

Periodical and Internet Sources Bibliography

The following articles have been selected to supplement the diverse views presented in this chapter.

Peter Bass, "The Economics of Gentrification," Culture and Youth Studies, March 2016. http://cultureandyouth.org/poverty/articles -poverty/the-economics-of-gentrification-2/.

Joe Cortright, "In Defense of Gentrification," *Atlantic*, October 31, 2015. https://www.theatlantic.com/business/archive/2015/10/in -defense-of-gentrification/413425/.

Economist, "Gentrification Is Good for the Poor," February 21, 2015. http://www.businessinsider.com/gentrification-is-good-for-the -poor-2015-2.

Daniel Fernández Méndez, "The Economics of Gentrification," Mises Institute, November 29, 2017. https://mises.org/wire/economics -gentrification.

Patrick Gillespie, "How Gentrification May Benefit the Poor," CNN Money, November 12, 2015. http://money.cnn.com/2015/11/12 /news/economy/gentrification-may-help-poor-people/index.html.

Daniel Herriges, "Who Benefits from Neighborhood Improvements?," Strong Towns, November 1, 2017. https://www.strongtowns.org /journal/2017/11/1/who-benefits-from-neighborhood -improvements.

John Muller, "Gentrification a Matter of Economics, Not Ethnicity," Greater Greater Washington, June 28, 2011. https://ggwash.org /view/9881/gentrification-a-matter-of-economics-not-ethnicity.

Barry Plunkett, Joe Novak, and William Lee, "Impacts of Gentrification: A Policy Primer," Penn Warton Public Policy Initiative, November 21, 2016. https://publicpolicy.wharton .upenn.edu/live/news/1581-impacts-of-gentrification-a-policy -primer/for-students/blog/news.php.

Dave Roos, "How Gentrification Works," HowStuffWorks, May 17, 2011. https://money.howstuffworks.com/gentrification.htm.

Timothy Taylor, "Economics of Gentrification," Conversable Economist, December 6, 2016. http://conversableeconomist .blogspot.com/2016/12/economics-of-gentrification_6.html.

For Further Discussion

Chapter 1
1. Do the improvements brought by gentrification benefit all residents of a neighborhood?
2. Is urban revitalization and renewal worth the negative aspects that come with it?
3. Is historic preservation an important reason for urban renewal, no matter what?

Chapter 2
1. Should there be blanket public policies to prevent the displacement of residents from gentrifying neighborhoods?
2. Could there ever be a situation in which it was not in the best interest of a landlord to displace existing rental tenants?
3. Does gentrification really create more diverse neighborhoods? Why or why not?

Chapter 3
1. How might a community's history and culture actually benefit from gentrification?
2. Explain how gentrification can reduce the crime rate in a neighborhood. Is this always true?
3. Can you think of another type of widespread ethnic neighborhood in American cities, besides a Chinatown, that might be impacted by gentrification?

Chapter 4
1. How can gentrification benefit schools and public services?
2. How does tourism relate to gentrification?
3. Who benefits the most economically from gentrification? Should there be policies to regulate profit from redevelopment?

Organizations to Contact

The editors have compiled the following list of organizations concerned with the issues debated in this book. The descriptions are derived from materials provided by the organizations. All have publications or information available for interested readers. The list was compiled on the date of publication of the present volume; the information provided here may change. Be aware that many organizations take several weeks or longer to respond to inquiries, so allow as much time as possible.

Habitat for Humanity International

121 Habitat St.
Americus, GA 31709-3498
(800) 422-4828
website: https://www.habitat.org

Habitat for Humanity partners with people and communities all over the world to revitalize housing and create communities that are vital, safe places for all people to live, now and in the future.

Main Street America

The National Main Street Center, Inc.
53 W. Jackson Blvd., Suite 350
Chicago, IL 60604
(312) 610-5611
email: mainstreet@savingplaces.org
website: https://www.mainstreet.org

Main Street America focuses on helping communities be inclusive and accessible, creating long-term economic improvement, and supporting locally owned businesses.

Mercy Housing

1999 Broadway, Suite 1000
Denver, CO 80202
(303) 830-3300
email: info@mercyhousing.org
website: https://www.mercyhousing.org

Mercy Housing is a national nonprofit organization working toward healthy communities where poverty is reduced and affordable housing is easily available.

Metropolitan Council on Housing

168 Canal St., 6th Floor
New York, NY 10013
(212) 979-6238
website: http://metcouncilonhousing.org/

The Metropolitan Council on Housing was founded over fifty years ago to fight for tenants' rights in New York City. The council organizes tenants to stand up for their individual rights, as well as advocates for better housing policies citywide.

National Community Reinvestment Coalition (NCRC)

740 Fifteenth St., Suite 400
Washington, DC 20005
(202) 628-8866
website: https://ncrc.org

The NCRC works with a network of national, regional, and local member organizations to advocate for fair banking, housing, and business. The coalition works with community leaders, policy makers, and financial institutions.

National Housing Conference (NHC)

1900 M St. NW
Washington, DC 20036
(202) 466-2121
website: https://www.nhc.org

The NHC educates the public, as well as politicians and decision makers, about the need for thriving communities with affordable, accessible, quality housing.

National Low Income Housing Coalition (NLIHC)

1000 Vermont Ave., Suite 500
Washington, DC 20005
(202) 662-1530
email: outreach@nlihc.org
website: http://nlihc.org/

The NLIHC works to achieve socially just policies that allow low-income people in the United States to have decent and affordable housing.

Neighborworks America

999 N. Capitol St. NE, Suite 900
Washington, DC 20002
(202) 760-4000
email: editor@nw.org
website: http://www.neighborworks.org

Neighborworks is involved in helping with community development and creating affordable housing by networking with 240 nationwide community development organizations.

Right to the City Alliance

388 Atlantic Ave.
Brooklyn, NY 11217
(844) 788-2489
email: info@righttothecity.org
website: https://righttothecity.org/

Right to the City Alliance was founded to create a unified response to issues like gentrification and the displacement of minorities. They work for racial justice, urban justice, human rights, and democracy.

Urban Institute

2100 M St. NW
Washington, DC 20037
(202) 833-7200
email: info@urban.org
website: https://www.urban.org/

The Urban Institute conducts economic and social policy research, including housing and family issues, and makes policy recommendations.

US Department of Housing and Urban Development

451 Seventh St. SW
Washington, DC 20410
(202) 708-1112
website: https://www.hud.gov

The US Department of Housing and Urban development is a government organization that works to create strong, sustainable communities that are inclusive and to make quality housing affordable for everyone.

Bibliography of Books

Japonica Brown-Saracino, *The Gentrification Debates: A Reader.* New York, NY: Routledge, 2010.

Matthew Desmond, *Evicted: Poverty and Profit in the American City.* New York, NY: Broadway Books, 2017.

DW Gibson, *The Edge Becomes the Center: An Oral History of Gentrification in the 21st Century.* New York, NY: Overlook Press, 2016.

Ryan Gravel, *Where We Want to Live: Reclaiming Infrastructure for a New Generation of Cities.* New York, NY: St Martin's Press, 2016.

Matt Hern, *What a City Is For: Remaking the Politics of Displacement.* Cambridge, MA: MIT Press, 2016.

Kay S. Hymowitz, *The New Brooklyn: What It Takes to Bring a City Back.* New York, NY: Rowman & Littlefield Publishers, 2017.

Jane Jacobs, *The Death and Life of Great American Cities.* New York, NY: Vintage Books, 1992.

Jerome Krase and Judith N. DeSena, *Race, Class, and Gentrification in Brooklyn: A View from the Street.* Lanham, MD: Lexington Books, 2018.

Loretta Lees, *The Gentrification Reader.* New York, NY: Routledge, 2010.

Loretta Lees, *Planetary Gentrification.* Boston, MA: Polity Press, 2016.

Loretta Lees and Martin Phillips, *Handbook of Gentrification Studies.* Cheltenham, UK: Edward Elger Publishing, 2018.

Loretta Lees, Hyun Bang Shin, and Ernesto López-Morales, *Global Gentrifications: Uneven Development and Displacement.* Bristol, UK: Policy Press, 2015.

Peter Marcuse and David Madden, *In Defense of Housing: The Politics of Crisis.* Brooklyn, NY: Verso, 2016.

Peter Moscowitz, *How to Kill a City: Gentrification, Inequality, and the Fight for the Neighborhood.* New York, NY: Nation Books, 2017.

Jeremiah Moss, *Vanishing New York: How a Great City Lost Its Soul.* New York, NY: Dey Street Books, 2017.

John Joe Schlichtman, Jason Patch, and Marc Lamont Hill, *Gentrifier.* Toronto: University of Toronto Press, 2017.

Index